148 Compressor intake
149 Generator
150 Runway emergency arrestor hook, lowered
151 Engine auxiliary air intake doors, open
152 Port hydraulic reservoir
153 Flap drive motor
154 Rear spar attachment main frame
155 Main undercarriage wheel bay
156 Flap shroud structure
157 Flap rib construction
158 Port plain flap
159 Trailing edge honeycomb panels
160 Aileron rib construction
161 Aileron tandem hydraulic jacks
162 Control cable linkages
163 Port aileron
164 Fixed portion of trailing edge
165 Port position light
166 AIM-9P Sidewinder air-to-air missile
167 Missile launch rail
168 Port outboard stores pylon
169 Pylon attachment hardpoints
170 Outer wing panel spars
171 Main undercarriage leg door
172 Port mainwheel
173 Inboard stores pylon
174 Main undercarriage leg strut
175 Hydraulic retraction jack
176 Undercarriage leg pivot fixing
177 Side locking breaker strut
178 Main undercarriage mounting rib
179 Wing panel multi-spar construction
180 Leading edge flap rib construction
181 Port leading edge manoeuvre flap

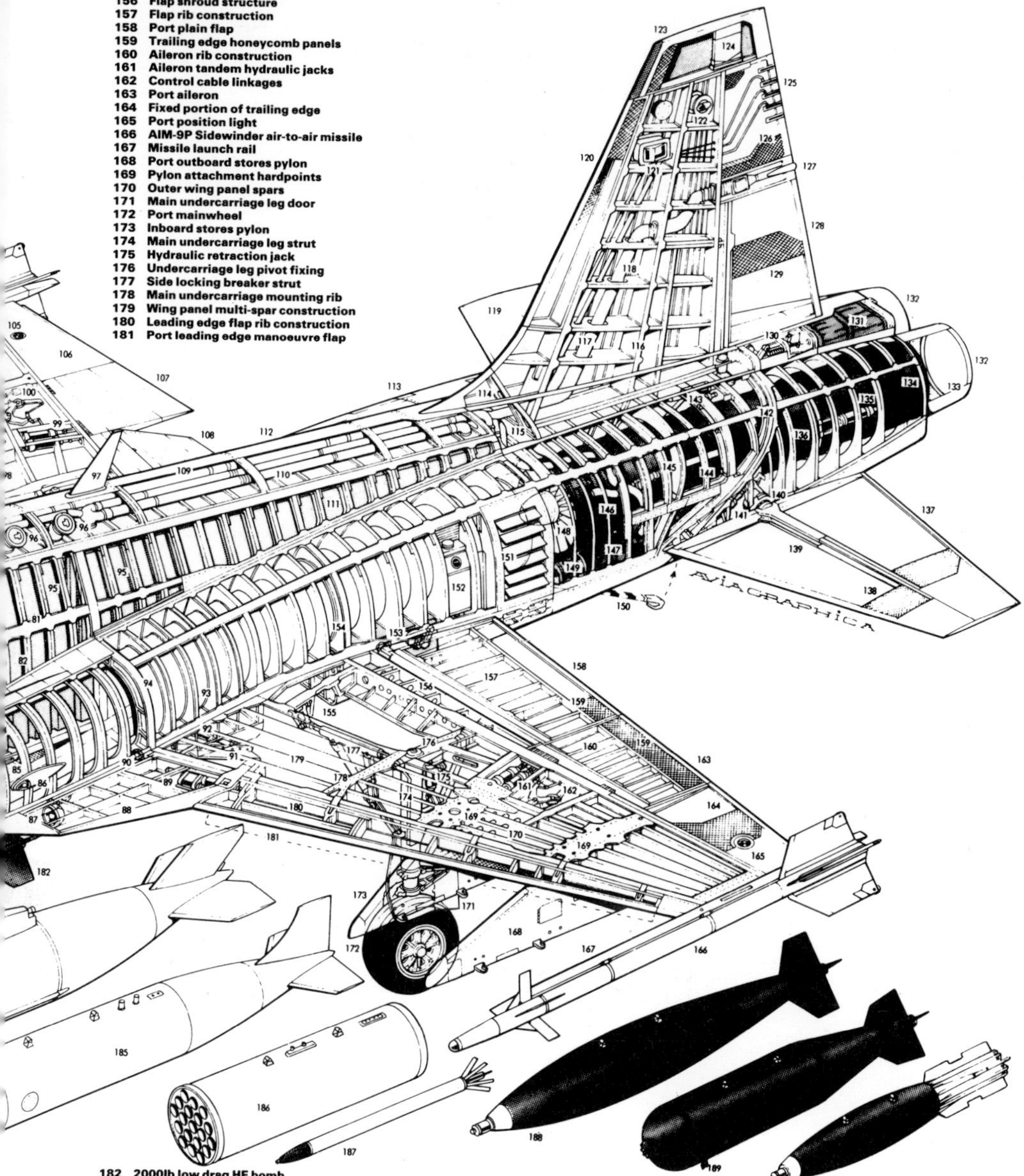

182 2000lb low drag HE bomb
183 Fuselage centreline pylon, 3,000lb (1,360kg) capacity
184 Centreline external fuel tank, 275 US gal (1,041 litres)
185 Wing pylon tank, 150 US gal (568 litres)
186 LAU-31A rocket pack, 19×2.75in ground attack rockets
187 2.75in (68mm) folding fin aircraft rocket (FFAR)
188 1,000lb (454kg) Mk83 HE bomb
189 CBU 24 or 49 cluster bomb
190 Snakeye retarded bomb

NORTHROP F-5/F-20

Northrop vastly improved the photo-reconnaissance capability of the F-5 with the RF-5E, one of which was itself photographed at Palmdale on 19 June 1979. The angle of the v-shaped image windows is emphasised here.

Chile became an F-5E customer in June 1978, the air force's Grupo 7 operating both variants. J-800 was the first F-5E (ex-75-442). *Northrop via Dorr*

Modern Combat Aircraft 25

NORTHROP F-5/F-20

Jerry Scutts

IAN ALLAN LTD
LONDON

Acknowledgements
A great number of references were consulted to piece together the history of the T-38 and F-5 and to these bones have been added the flesh in the form of photographs and data from equally numerous organisations and individuals. To them all I extend grateful thanks for their time and effort. They include: Robert F. Dorr; Dana Bell; Bruce Robertson; Barry Wheeler; Jim Corfield and Ira E. Chart of Northrop; Canadair; Mike Hooks; George Pennick; Dave Menard; Jim Mesko; Harry Siepmann; Roger Warren; the staff of the Civil Aviation Authority library, who put up with the transfer of vast amounts of their references to my office for long periods of time; Trish M. Field of *Canadian Aviation*; Yan Whytlaw of FAI; the Public Affairs Office of NASA's Ames Research Center; the US Department of Defense and the US Air Force. Unless otherwise credited the illustrations are reproduced courtesy of Northrop.

United States distribution by

Motorbooks International
Publishers & Wholesalers Inc
Osceola, Wisconsin 54020, USA ®

First published 1986

ISBN 0 7110 1576 7

Published by Ian Allan Ltd, Shepperton, Surrey; and printed by Ian Allan Printing Ltd at their works at Coombelands in Runnymede, England

Contents

Preface

One of the most successful military aircraft series of modern times, the Northrop F-5 fighters and T-38 trainers have been in service for over three decades. A radical departure from established American combat aircraft design thinking, these lightweight machines of the mid-1950s set new standards in pilot training in the art of supersonic flight and gave the world's air forces a reliable interceptor/ground attack type at a time when it was urgently required.

Anyone looking into the development and sales success of Northrop Corporation's major aerospace product of recent times will realise that the best-selling F-5 has not found its markets without a degree of controversy. As a key element of the US Military Assistance Programme support of foreign governments, the aircraft had to be thoroughly proven to the American military establishment before being accepted for production. It had also to weather considerable opposition to the entire concept of lightweight fighters — and it subsequently took centre stage in numerous rows when yesterday's friendly nation became tomorrow's political embarrassment.

But with a winning design, Northrop withstood all the brickbats and got on with the job of producing the aircraft that a great many people wanted. And if the customer suddenly became persona non grata the company switched its sales pitch to others — indeed there were few nations that were not approached during Northrop's intensive sales drive for the F-5.

To some countries that acquired the F-5, it was more than just another combat aircraft; it became little short of a ticket to political stability in the eyes of the West. It meant membership of the 'Free World' and US confirmation that the government of the day had at least some semblance of democracy. That some of these political facades could crumble with startling rapidity was shown most dramatically by Iran and Vietnam, but quieter external pressures could have equally traumatic results, as Nationalist China found with the United Nations' recognition of Red China. All these events affected the world inventory of the Northrop F-5.

One could therefore write a substantial book on the political background to F-5 sales. But this lies largely outside the scope of a technical development history and I have touched on the subject only briefly and where necessary to maintain continuity.

Thirty years would seem to be more than enough time for someone to write a comprehensive account of the T-38/F-5; quite why nobody has is difficult to determine, but I am pleased to fill the gap with this, the first hardback book record. There are future chapters of the story still to be added, for the Talon and Tiger have long lives ahead of them. And if their lineage is perpetuated in production models of the descendant F-20 Tigershark, the final record will be substantial. The following narrative is perhaps, two-thirds along the way.

Jerry Scutts

1 A Fresh Approach

During the 1950s a number of aerospace companies, concerned over the increasing complexity and spiralling cost of front line military aircraft, turned their attention to simpler, cheaper technology and attempted to design aircraft that would be attractive to nations with modest defence budgets. It was also hoped that such aircraft would find a good home market at a time when nations faced an increasing threat — real or imagined — from growing Communist expansion. The availability of cheaper combat aircraft would enable such nations to buy in substantial numbers, rather than be forced to maintain more limited forces if they were obliged to purchase the highly sophisticated and costly types then being planned, particularly in Britain, France and the USA. At that time many countries also faced a quantum leap from subsonic first generation jets to the supersonic age, bringing challenges not only in pilot training but in the provision of adequate base facilities with skilled personnel to maintain the new machines to the required standard of readiness.

If European air forces committed to NATO experienced this 'technology gap' then SEATO forces on the other side of the world were if anything even worse off, equipped as they were with largely obsolescent US equipment of the World War 2 period. Asia, the Middle East, Africa and the richer areas of Latin America were where potentially vast markets for military equipment lay, and Britain, France and Italy were among the countries that explored lightweight fighters and trainers in an attempt to supply them. The key word was 'lightweight': it was estimated that a small airframe with a total weight below 20,000lb would meet most requirements.

In the UK, the tiny Folland concern developed the nimble Midge single-seater; Italy's Aerfer Sagittario 2 was the culmination of light fighter tradition stretching back some 20 years; and France responded to a 1954 NATO lightweight fighter competition with the Breguet 10001 Taon. The competition was generated by General Louis Norstad's staff and issued to European industry in April of that year.

The NATO contest was based on ideas put forward by Folland designer W. E. W. Petter as early as 1950, and it helped bring some of these European designs as far as prototype flight testing. But the concept proved to be too far ahead of its time, only the Midge achieving limited series production in single-seat form, as the Gnat.

Initially there was little interest in lightweight fighters on the other side of the Atlantic, US industry being content to concentrate on the large and increasingly complex aircraft that were pushing forward the 'state of the art'. Only the small Northrop Corporation of Hawthorne, California seriously explored the lightweight combat aircraft and by independently funding the necessary research, was eventually to lead the field in America. With the F-89 Scorpion in the last stages of production the N-156 series became Northrop's major aerospace project of the 1960s; it represented faith in an idea — and no little dogged determination to see it through to production, high sales and an outstanding achievement. In the fullness of time Northrop was to produce one of the most successful of modern combat aircraft with a reliability record second to none.

In order to determine the requirements for future economical fighters in the Free World, in 1954 Northrop despatched a team of management and technical personnel to Europe and Asia. From discussions there came, understandably, a set of requirements differing widely in detail. But they gave the American team a sound basis on which to plan a lightweight fighter calculated to cost about half as much as, for example, any of the 'Century' series of fighters then in the planning stage by the larger US manufacturers. In order to meet diverse requirements for intercept, ground attack/close support and interdiction by land based air forces — as well as the needs of navies with carrier capability — Northrop conceived a family of aircraft under the project number N-156.

The programme had its origins in December 1952, when Edgar Schmued (previously with North American Aviation and whose design work had included the superlative P-51 Mustang), Northrop Vice President in charge of Engineering, initiated a design study for a relatively simple, lightweight supersonic fighter. The preliminary design team for the project, under the designation N-102, was headed by Welko Gasich, Chief of Advanced Design. Lee Begin, later Northrop's

Vice President for Advanced Programmes and Planning, was then working 'at the drawing board'. The new design was given the name Fang.

The Fang emerged as a delta with an anhedral slab type tailplane, powered by a single turbojet situated in the lower aft fuselage and fed via a large ventral intake employing variable geometry. It was in the 15,000-18,000lb AUW class depending on stores carried and was planned as a Mach 2 interceptor with several advanced feature in a rugged, simple airframe. The 30ft 8in span wing was of thin section with pronounced conical camber on the leading edges, shoulder mounted and incorporating two stores stations.

Retention of a tailplane on a delta planform was a departure from traditional US practice, as was the location of the air intake. A single powerplant of the General Electric J79, Pratt & Whitney J57 or Wright J65 size was envisaged.

Northrop began work on the Fang towards the end of 1952 and had a complete mock-up built by late 1954, by which time design studies had been completed for a tandem two-seat training version. This required a fuselage stretch to 45ft 2½in compared with the fighter's 42ft 10in. Eight different armament installations were proposed for the Fang fighter including a rotary Vulcan gun. The Fang mock-up was given the serial number 52-2777.

One drawback foreseen was the use of a large, conventional turbojet: not only would this require a large amount of fuel, but its cost would be high. This factor was one of the primary reasons for cancellation of further work on the Fang. Tom Jones, then Northrop Planning Officer (later President and Chief Executive) felt that this was not the way the company should go. He pressed for a reassessment of the fighter programme, with more emphasis on keeping the cost down.

At this point, Northrop's brainchild was helped considerably by the availability of very small turbojets being produced primarily for guided missiles. With very high thrust to weight ratios and dimensions modest enough to fit into a very compact fighter airframe, these engines became the crux of the aircraft Northrop was planning. All further designs were therefore based on two J85 engines then being developed by General Electric for the USAF's GAM-72 Green Quail decoy missile.

The Northrop team progressed to the 'Tally-ho' project, which had two turbojets in pods under a mid-fuselage unswept wing. The subject of a March 1955 study labelled N-156TX, the aircraft also had a very long one-piece cockpit canopy over tandem seats, and a low-set tailplane. It was the most radical departure of the studies Northrop came up with during N-156 planning.

Projected performance figures for the TX were disappointing and the design team moved on to the N-156NN naval fighter. This aircraft, not unlike the Grumman Panther in configuration, brought the two engines into the fuselage, each one being fed by separate air intakes flanking the cockpit sidewalls.

Strengthened for shipboard operation and incorporating carrier launch and recovery equipment, the N-156NN also had a T-tail, full span trailing edge flaps and provision for a tractor-type landing gear. Emerging in November 1955 as Project Design PD-2706, the navalised version of the N-156 family was curtailed primarily by the

Below:
Although the N-102 Fang bore little resemblance to the N-156 it was the first tangible design to emerge from the lengthy series of studies that preceded the F-5 forerunners.

mothballing of the US Navy's escort carrier fleet. An escort size carrier had been envisaged by Northrop for the N-156NN, principally American, but not forgetting the ships of other navies. The company offered the fighter as being compatible with the British 'Majestic' class ships, six of which had been laid down in 1943.

By 1955, one 'Majestic' was in service with Australia (with a second commissioning that year) and Canada had one, with a second due for delivery in two years' time. India's single 'Majestic' class carrier would also enter service in 1957. These 14,000-ton light fleet carriers would operate jet strike aircraft and fighters and,

following a US Navy launch order, might well have been equipped with Northrop designs, leading the Californian company down a different path. But it was not to be.

Although not entirely abandoning a carrier-based fighter, Northrop henceforth concentrated on land-planes of modest proportions with low weight, mostly with two seats and offering a useful dual role as fighter/trainers. The exercise went through another series of studies, seven configurations emerging in 1956. Six had project design numbers as follows: PD-2821 (announced in January 1956); PD-2832 (March); PD-2879A (May); PD-2879B (October); and PD-2879D (December). The last of these two-seaters more or less established the final shape for aerodynamic wind tunnel testing, for which 14 models were used primarily to determine the degree of area ruling the fuselage needed.

In October 1956 a seventh design introduced the N-156 designation that was used for the direct forerunners of the T-38/F-5 series. This was the single-seat N156F, PD-2879D becoming the N-156T. Northrop submitted the trainer variant to the USAF in March 1956, in response to a General Operational Requirement issued in 1955 for a supersonic trainer. Air Training Command was then looking for an aircraft to replace its ageing fleet of Lockheed T-33s, the project being an attractive prospect for manufacturers who could anticipate high volume production.

In June 1956 it was announced that the N-156T had been selected for purchase, pending successful prototype flight testing. The USAF authorised three prototypes (58-1191 to 58-1193 including the latter as a static test airframe) under the

Below:

With its contrived serial number, the N-156 mock-up reflected the general configuration of the T-38 and F-5, it being modified to single-seat form during the N-156F design studies.

Bottom:

The transformed mock-up was examined by the USAF and Department of Defense in 1958. Note the T-38-type air intakes and the dummy missiles on the wingtips.

designation YT-38. The name Talon was chosen.

The wing area of the N-156T was established at 170sq ft (down from the 216sq ft of previous design studies), a slightly revised wing with equal taper of both leading and trailing edges giving an aspect ratio of 4.75. The vertical tail surfaces were increased to 27sq ft (from 17sq ft) when the ventral fin was dropped. Also shelved at an early stage was a mechanically-drooping nose which was intended to increase visibility from the second seat — one drawback with earlier generation trainers was that the pupil and instructor sat in seats at the same level. Deemed to be too heavy and complex, the drooped nose was not proceeded with, although Northrop did set the second (instructor's) seat 10in higher, enabling a useful 'over the shoulder' view of the front seat occupant. These revisions to the N-156T were incorporated into a full-scale mock-up with the spurious serial number '55-6156', and widely referred to simply as the 'TZ'.

An all-metal low wing cantilever monoplane employing area ruling which gave a distinctive 'waisting' of the fuselage at mid-position, the T-38A offered a high safety factor from two engines. It was envisaged that each General Electric J85 GE-5 turbojet would give a rated thrust of 2,500lb and 3,650lb with afterburning. Each engine also had an independent fuel system, the port one taking its supply from forward fuselage and dorsal tanks positioned aft of the second cockpit, that on the starboard side being fed from centre and rear fuselage tanks. Total fuel capacity was 580 US gallons, all stored in the fuselage.

A fully powered rudder was fitted and the low-set tailplane was a one-piece, all-moving unit. There were no wing or tail trim tabs, the ailerons being powered; the aircraft was not fitted with a braking parachute, although there were two air brakes on the underside of the fuselage forward of the mainwheel wells.

The T-38's cockpit was pressurised and air conditioned, there being separate rearwards-hinging jettisonable canopies over both seats. Positioned well forward of the wing, the cockpits provided excellent visibility to both occupants and all controls were located forward of the pilot's normal elbow position, thereby reducing significantly the possibility of procedural errors by the student pilot. The flight envelope included full aerobatic, night and instrument flying as well as cross country navigation using TACAN and ILS marker beacon, with UHF command radio for communications.

Northrop built considerable strength into the aircraft; the tricycle undercarriage had a wide track, a steerable nosewheel aided stability on the ground, and the design of the landing gear enabled operation from 'unprepared' surfaces. Either engine provided power for the hydraulics for the flight controls; aileron and rudder 'feel' was achieved by control force springs operating with bob weights. Longitudinal and directional stability augmenters were installed in series with the control system.

In the meantime, General Electric was experiencing severe problems with the J85 engine. Cramer 'Jim' LaPierre, the company's vice president and general manager of the Aircraft Gas Turbine Division, had visited Northrop to discuss the J85's prospects with Ed Schmued and Welko Gasich. LaPierre assured the Northrop men that GE could achieve the required output and advised the company to go ahead with the N-156F fighter project based around the J85 powerplant. The trouble was the time needed to refine the engine to acceptable standards. The USAF finally lost patience and gave GE and Northrop an ultimatum — fly the T-38 by 11 April 1959 or forget the J85 programme.

As it was impossible to instal an afterburning J85-5 engine in time for the first flight, the YT-38 (58-1191) was moved to Edwards Air Force Base early in April fitted with a pair of YJ85-1s offering only 1,900lb st each. GE Engine Group Engineering boss Ed Woll meanwhile put a veritable task force to work on solving the J85's problems, anticipating that the new trainer would be the subject of volume production once the first test flights had been made.

On 10 April 1959 Chief Engineering Test Pilot Lew Nelson lifted the sleek trainer prototype from the Edwards runway. It took only a few minutes to realise that Northrop had a winner, despite the under-powered engines. The flight lasted 42 minutes during which time the aircraft reached a speed of Mach 0.9 and a height of 35,000ft. When he landed Nelson said, 'The T-38 is a clean airplane — the cleanest first flight in my experience. And the first with no squawks',

Five days later the YT-38 achieved Mach 1 in a shallow dive. The J85-1 also powered the second aircraft (58-1192) which flew on 12 June and it was not until the following January that the third aircraft to fly joined the test programme with the J85-5 engines installed. This was 58-1194, the first production T-38A-10-NO.

The first five production T-38As had uprated engines although General Electric retained the test status identifier 'YJ' until the J85 was cleared for series production. Capt Swart Nelson had become the first USAF pilot to fly a T-38 by the time Northrop received the initial order for four aircraft. This was in October 1959 and a further 13 were ordered before the end of the year.

2 Freedom Fighter

Although USAF interest in the trainer variant of the N-156 family brought some change of emphasis in the project for Northrop, Welko Gasich and his team continued work on the single-seat international fighter. Lee Begin's drawings reflected the high degree of commonality between the two aircraft and with T-38 development data to hand, progress was rapid. Having finalised the configuration of the N-156F, Northrop set out to incorporate those features most required by potential foreign customers of a lightweight small fighter and at the same time make it attractive enough to be entered for any industry competition the USAF might hold to find the best available aircraft for the programme.

One of the principles Northrop worked to with the N-156F was that it should be easily maintained even with the minimum of support facilities. Special attention was paid to simplifying engine overhaul and servicing, the aft section of the rear fuselage being a removable 'sleeve'. This one-piece section, with a distinctive forward-angled join line, gave easy access to the engines' centre and afterburner sections. Handling of engines was also facilitated by the fitting of an overhead track and trolley arrangement in each bay, and the hydraulic pump and generator with an engine-driven gearbox was a packaged unit mounted on the airframe. Alternate engines were also specified, among them the Pratt & Whitney J60 (JT12) and the Rolls-Royce RB145.

General Electric's development problems with the J85 were due mainly to its design as a 'dry' (without afterburning) powerplant which worked well enough as a missile engine, but considerably more work was necessary to adapt it to produce higher thrust: it was only the second small engine GE had produced.

In order to provide what amounted to nearly 70% more thrust, GE began work on the troublesome compressor and turbine sections which had almost led to cancellation of the entire programme prior to the first flight of the YT-38.

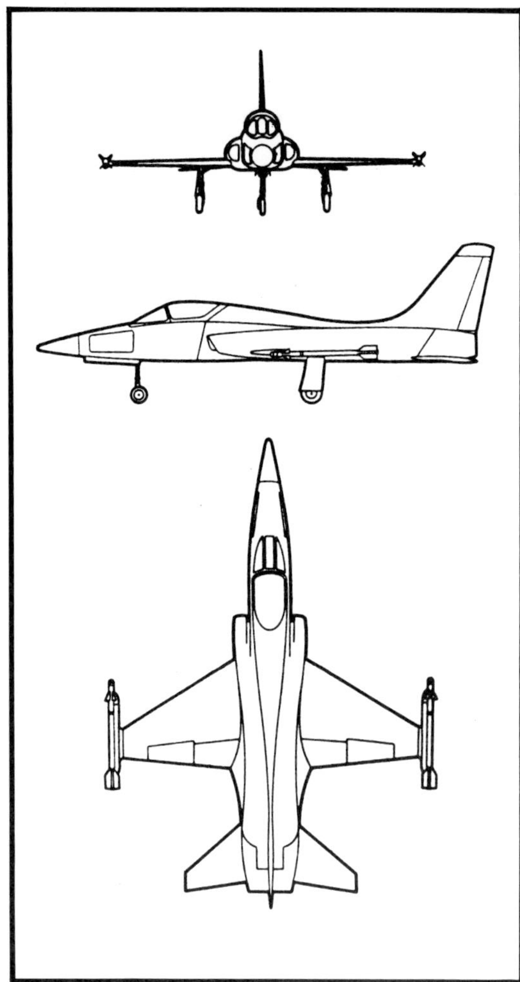

With Northrop proceeding with construction of the first N-156F, there was little choice but to instal another pair of J85-1s of 3,850lb thrust each.

Incorporating the high lift devices developed for the trainer, the N-156F had a similar wing but with a forward-angled fillet or LEX (leading edge extension) at each root. The wing had the same span as that of the YT-38 without tip tanks, and installation of these increased span to 25ft 10in. The removable tip tanks were characteristically area ruled or 'waisted' and held 50gal each. With internal fuel and tip tanks the aircraft lifted 683gal, or 1,133gal with two drop tanks under the wings, giving a maximum range of more than 2,300 miles. Northrop also incorporated into the design provision for an in-flight refuelling system using the fixed probe receiver and trailing drogue transfer technique.

Also included were locating points for JATO; the 1950s saw many experiments in the rocket-boosting of combat aircraft from ramps, both to save fuel and to eliminate the need to taxi to conventional (and vulnerable) runways. Additionally it was thought that boosters would enable fighters to use dispersed, unprepared sites. If necessary the N-156F could have been launched from such sites.

One feature that came to be standard on many F-5s was a tail hook for use with a runway arrester system. Designed for operating with hydraulic gear, the single-strut hook retracted to lie flat along the underside of the rear fuselage between the tailpipes. A more conventional back-up braking system was a 15ft diameter parachute, stowed in a box fairing at the base of the rudder. Using the drag chute the aircraft was designed to land with a ground roll of less than 1,800ft.

Primary armament of the N-156F was a combination of two 20mm M-39 cannon and the AIM-9 Sidewinder AAM on each wingtip station attached to Aero launchers for the basic intercept mission, with a range of bombs, missiles and rockets for ground attack. Among the stores specified were the Nord AS.30 air-to-ground missile and GAM-83A Bullpup, both of which required visual target acquisition and radio link guidance. A Hughes Mk II 20mm gun pod with a twin-barrel revolver cannon could alternatively be carried on the centreline pylon which was limited to a weight of 2,000lb. Initial N-156F configuration included only two wing stores stations limited to 1,000lb weight.

In keeping with the multi-role concept of the N-156 family, Northrop specified a camera nose which could be substituted rapidly for the standard fighter nose but without the need to remove the gun armament. This version was in fact intended to be a true dual-purpose day fighter, and was known as the N-156C.

Further studies into a version with a larger wing, more fuel capacity, greater payload and strengthened arrester gear for carrier operation were labelled N-156D. This was the penultimate attempt to create a navalised version, which Northrop kept 'on the back burner' for some years and in 1965 offered to the Royal Australian Navy as the N-285B. This development of the N156F was also made known to the US Navy in what is believed to have been the last of the company's design studies into a carrier-borne lightweight fighter. Northrop's design department also looked ahead to the F-5E when it produced studies for the N-156E, based around GE CF-700 aft fan engines giving 6,800lb st.

Department of Defense/USAF inspection of the reconfigured N-156 single-seat mock-up took place early in 1958, following which Northrop received authorisation to build three prototypes (59-4987 to 59-4989); a letter of intent dated 25 February 1958 also covered the construction of one static test

Bottom:
The first YF-5A pictured during its maiden flight on 30 July 1959. *via Bruce Robertson*

Below:
Capt A. J. Borgstein, of the Royal Netherlands Air Force became the first foreign pilot to fly the N-156F, in September 1959. Here Capt Borgstein enthuses over the new aircraft's performance with Lew Nelson, Northrop chief engineering test pilot (left), and Capt Swart Nelson after his 50-minute flight at Edwards. *via Robertson*

Below right:
The first N-156F conducted an extensive evaluation of external stores during the 33 months that were to elapse from first flight to the confirmation of production. Sidewinders and drop tanks were among the combinations. *Robertson*

Bottom right:
Weapons evaluation included maximum bomb load, 59-4987 carrying 18×250lb bombs here. The sales literature actually specified three on the wing pylons rather than six, the inboard station being stressed for 1,000lb. *Barry Wheeler*

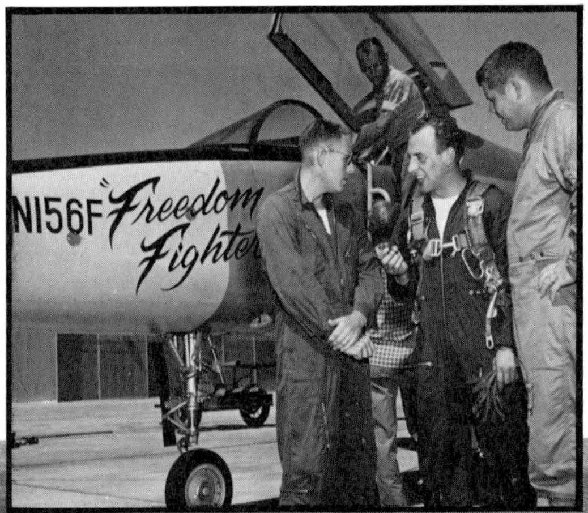

airframe, 59-4993. The prototypes were funded by the Air Force under the FX programme in support of the Military Assistance Programme (MAP) for a primarily 'counter-air' fighter. Having a good idea of the size of production run the chosen FX fighter could enjoy — through both MAP donations to friendly governments and sales through the Foreign Military Sales programme — Northrop proceeded apace with construction of the N-156F prototype, using as much T-38 tooling as practicable to shorten completion time.

In the meantime the company sought further confirmation of fighter aircraft requirements overseas; early in 1959 Northrop president W. C. Collins announced publicly that discussions were underway with countries showing an interest in licence production of the N-156F. The companies concerned included SABCA of Belgium, Fokker of Holland (in which Northrop had a 25% holding) and Fiat of Italy. Talks also took place with Australia and the UK — where Fairey Aviation gave some consideration to manufacturing both land-based and shipboard versions powered by the RB145.

Northrop's president went on record as saying that, 'Interest in this weapon is so extensive that we estimate its potential world-wide production as well in excess of 4,000 aircraft'. Even if a little optimistic, these prophetic words were tinged, as it transpired, with some irony — because although Belgium, Holland and Italy *were* to licence-build an American fighter, it was not to be the Northrop design but the N-156F's nearest rival in the FX competition, the Lockheed F-104.

To reflect the raison d'etre of the new fighter it was given the name Freedom Fighter and was duly

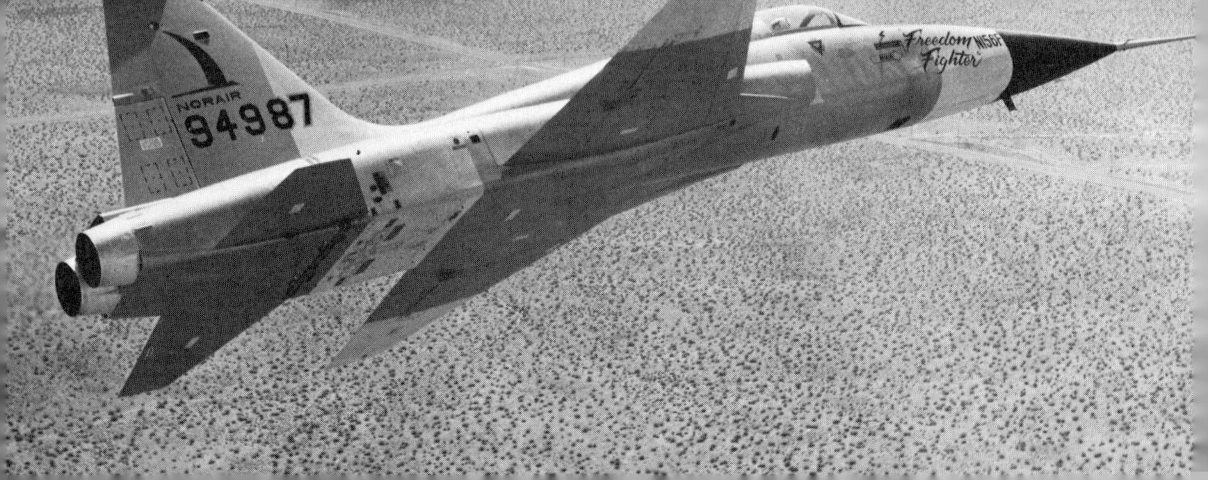

decorated with it before the first flight, along with liberal areas of high visibility day-glo paint. No armament was fitted. Lew Nelson was again at the controls of a Northrop prototype which took off from Edwards on 30 July 1959, barely four months after the maiden flight of the first prototype Talon. The single-seater bettered the performance of its stablemate by a considerable margin, despite the fact that the powerplants were once again the J85-1s. During those auspicious 50 minutes Nelson pushed the N-156F through Mach 1 and afterwards said it 'performed like a well-educated lady throughout the entire test'.

With a fighter prototype flying and construction of the second aircraft well advanced, Northrop passed an important milestone, and years of self-funding the N-156 project appeared to have been well worth the effort. Nevertheless, the fighter still had to be selected for production; not only did it face a potentially strong challenge from Lockheed, but it was obliged to weather considerable opposition to the entire concept of lightweight economy fighters then prevailing in some US circles. The concept had already proved to be too radical a departure from established practice elsewhere, certainly in Britain, where the Folland Gnat (notwithstanding excellent potential) found very little official support. Other European companies also had difficulty in convincing their respective governments to back lightweight fighters and in the event only the Gnat progressed beyond the prototype stage.

The USAF was reported to have a marked preference for a 'limited capability' version of the F-104 Starfighter to fulfil FX specifications. It was estimated that by removing the advanced all-weather fire control and navigation system and thereby making the aircraft somewhat simpler to maintain and cheaper to operate, the F-104 might be an attractive buy. Not everyone agreed with this reasoning but the Air Force nevertheless strongly backed Lockheed's projected MAP version, alternatively known as the F-104-17 or F-104H/ TF-104H fighter/trainer.

In its turn Northrop enjoyed the support of the Department of Defense's International Security

Affairs Agency (ISAA) which would make the final choice. ISAA was of the opinion that the N-156F was better suited to MAP requirements.

Northrop completed and flew the second N-156F (59-4988) but decided to suspend work on the third aircraft until the DoD decided whether it merited a production contract. Further development at that stage meant digging even deeper into the company purse, possibly without any orders with which to recoup costs. But with two aircraft flying Northrop was able to complete further flight tests and performance trials including in-the-field maintenance and rough-strip operating. While the first prototype did most of the early test flying, including carriage and release of a full range of stores, the second machine carried out unprepared field tests. A turnround time of less than eight minutes was achieved in these latter operations, which took place in June 1961 at Pensacola, Florida and included landing within 1,300ft on grass and taking off with maximum fuel load within a distance of 2,500ft.

With flight tests complete, Northrop temporarily halted the N-156F programme, but in early January 1962 an Army requirement for a new close-support fixed wing aircraft saw the first prototype engaged in a further series of trials. The Army supplied pilots for comparative tests with the A-4D-2N Skyhawk, the Fiat G-91 and the N-156F, held at Edwards for some two months. The Northrop aircraft was temporarily given 'Army' markings for the duration of the evaluation.

The USAF took a keen interest in the outcome of these tests, noting that the Army liked the N-156F's performance under limited warfare conditions and commented very favourably on its maintainability and operational readiness. It was further thought that the aircraft's unusually small frontal area coupled with very small engine intakes would significantly reduce its chances of being fatally hit during ground attack runs.

But at that time, the whole question of Army close support was building up to a bitter argument with the Air Force. The Army was denied jurisdiction over this class of warfare — at least in the use of its own fixed-wing aircraft — by the DoD, and the competition was cancelled. In the event the Army chose helicopters for its own air support and the Air Force kept responsibility for fixed-wing support.

Right:
The hard-working first aircraft seen during the Army close support evaluation in 1962, complete with that service's markings.

Below:
The first and third YF-5As take-off from Edwards for Sidewinder trials. Note the partially-painted Air Force designator on '987.

3 White Rocket

While Northrop awaited the decision on the future of the N-156F, the T-38 was prepared to embark on a service career which would be second to none in terms of reliability and cost-effectiveness. By the autumn of 1959 the first two prototypes had completed 100 flights with no major problems encountered. Milt Kuska, Edwards' Director of Flight Test Engineering, stated that the YT-38 required no aerodynamic changes at all during the entire programme — an unprecedented record for a supersonic aircraft. The YT-38s were also building a reputation for outstanding flight characteristics; they were extremely forgiving of mistakes and also commendably low on maintenance time.

In October the USAF contracted for a further 50 Talons, the order including a provision for output to be raised from two to 10 aircraft per month — which Northrop improved upon in 1961 by building 12 T-38s every month. In 1958 the company had introduced the new 'Norail' moving assembly line which greatly speeded output at Hawthorne.

The flight test programme was completed in February 1961 after 2,000 flights had been made. The USAF announced that it had been the most successful in the history of the Flight Test Centre. Eight Air Force pilots had flown each phase of the tests, using both YT-38s and five early production machines. Test instrumentation occupied the rear seat for a number of flights, the installed package including an oscillograph, photo-panel, signal conditioning equipment and a camera.

The success of the test programme was a tribute to Northrop's extreme thoroughness in the design and construction phases, the T-38 having been subject to more wind tunnel testing than any aircraft previously. In consequence very few changes were made on production aircraft — or throughout the Talon's entire history. Production machines did however have a number of features that distinguished them from the prototypes, including an underside curved metal plate over the exhaust nozzles, and an air intake to cool the afterburners set on the fuselage top, flanking the fin fillet.

By August 1961 the order book for the T-38A had been boosted by another 144 aircraft, and Northrop secured the first of a dozen performance records for its star newcomer. Renowned woman

Below:
The striking colour scheme of NASA has been worn by 30 T-38s to date, this one being in service at the Ames Research Centre. *NASA*

Left:
The YT-38A seen soon after roll-out contrasts sharply with the N-156F mock-up. *Wheeler*

Bottom left:
Annotated diagram showing the front cockpit of an early production T-38A-20, 59-1602, the first of the third production batch.

1. Vertical Situation Display
2. Horizontal Situation Display
3. Master Caution Light
4. Altimeter
5. Canopy Lock Light
6. Vertical speed Indicator
7. Tachometers
8. Temperature Exhaust Indicators
9. Nozzle Position Indicators
10. Right Fire Warning Light
11. Oil Pressure Indicators
12. Fuel Quantity Indicators
13. Fuel Control Panel
14. Canopy Jettison 'T' Handle
15. Torso Air Outlet
16. Liquid Oxygen Quantity Indicator
17. Warning Lights Panel
18. Oxygen Regulator
19. Fuel Flow Indicators
20. Flight Control Hydraulic Pressure Indicator
21. Utility Hydraulic Pressure Indicator
22. Communication Panel
23. Tacan Tactical Air Navigation Panel
24. ILS (Instrument Landing System) Panel
25. Intercom Selector Panel
26. Communication and Navigation Override Panel
27. Air Start Switch
28. Flap Position Indicator
29. Landing Gear Control Panel
30. Left Fire Warning Light
31. Accelerometer
32. Navigation Mode Selector Panel
33. Aircraft Clock
34. Mach Airspeed Indicator
35. Marker Beacon Light

Above:
By contrast, an excellent view of the second seat, panel and controls of 60-549, a T-38A-25.

Below:
Test pilot Lew Nelson kitted up and ready to fly the No 1 YT-38.

pilot Jacqueline Cochran, who had previously become the first aviatrix to fly faster than the speed of sound, began the record series on 24 August. (See Appendix 1 for details.) Flying a production T-38, she set eight records, including six for a woman pilot, the last being flown on 12 October.

The following February Maj Walter F. Daniel of the Air Force used T-38A 61-849 to establish four new time-to-climb records, flying from both Edwards and Pt Mugu NAS. Figures were submitted to the FAI for times to reach 3,000, 6,000, 9,000 and 12,000m. Each one beat the previous record by an F-104A made in December 1958 by the required 3%, the fastest being the 12,000m (39,272ft) climb, which took the Talon a mere 94.74 seconds from 'brakes off'.

In May 1964 the National Aeronautics & Space Administration accepted the first of 30 T-38s which were to serve the agency in a number of roles, paramount among which was to maintain the flight proficiency of astronauts. Many of these men had already flown the T-38 as part of their military training and two, Neil Armstrong and Elliot See, had been involved in the development programmes for the Talon and F-5. Armstrong was one of the NASA pilots who flew early F-5 tests and See had previously been a T-38 project test pilot with Northrop.

See was killed in a T-38 early in 1966 when the aircraft he was flying with fellow astronaut Charles Bassett crashed into the McDonnell building in St Louis. See took off from Ellington AFB near the Johnson Space Center to visit the McDonnell plant, in company with another T-38 flown by astronauts Tom Sheppard and Gene Cernan. See's aircraft ran into fog at St Louis, stalled on approach and hit the McDonnell building, coming to rest in a car park with both crewmen dead. Stafford and Cernan replaced their colleagues as prime crew for Gemini 9.

This was the second T-38 accident to claim the lives of astronauts; the first happened in 1964 when Ted Freeman's aircraft crashed after hitting a snow goose. In 1967 Clifton Williams lost aileron control and hit the ground at Mach 1 plus.

In NASA service the T-38s all wore civil registrations on their predominantly white finish with coloured trim. They supplemented T-33s and other types for training and general hack work, astronauts often having to commute long distances across the USA. These flights were often completed with one engine shut down to conserve fuel, the pilots invariably wearing back pack parachutes as the seat pan of the ejector seat conveniently housed a specifically-designed overnight case for personal belongings.

Being young and among the nation's best pilots, the astronauts often raced each other in their hot

U.S. AIR FORCE
USAF
81191
TF-191
U.S. AIR FORCE
T-38 TALON
81192

little Talons, strictly unofficially. Supersonic flights over land were commonplace and many T-38 tyres were burst as pilots stamped on the brakes to shorten the landing roll and be first at the ramp. Frank Borman was also notorious for his 'hot refuelling' — putting the juice in with the J85s running to save time.

The many support roles requiring regular use of aircraft by the armed services, NASA and the aerospace manufacturers saw the T-38 become a familiar sight at air bases and research centres throughout the USA. Among these were: Wright-Patterson AFB (range support); Los Angeles International Airport (USAF programme support); Lockheed-Marietta (C-5 programme support) and Langley AFB (NASA support), to name but very few.

Fairly routine though these duties may have been, the task of chaseplane on prototype test flights is not without risk, as the pilots of a F-5 and a T-38 had starkly demonstrated to them in June 1966. Up with a four-ship chase element otherwise comprising a F-4 Phantom and a F-104 formating with the second prototype XB-70 Valkyrie, they watched with horror as the F-104 came into contact with the XB-70's tail. The Valkyrie was totally destroyed in the ensuing crash, as was the Starfighter and although the Phantom and both Northrop types landed safely, there were some anxious moments during that tragic flight.

For years all USAF and NASA T-38s operated in a predominantly white paint scheme with standardised markings — leading to the appropriate nickname 'White Rocket'. Similar markings were also adopted for all the Talons purchased by West Germany and paid for in Deutschmarks for the Luftwaffe Starfighter training programme.

Following an initial evaluation of the T-38A by a group of Luftwaffe pilots under the command of wartime fighter ace Col Gunther Rall, six German instructors took a T-38 familiarisation course in December 1962 in anticipation of a sizeable order for the Talon and Cessna T-37 by Germany. It was then realised that there was a substantial advantage in basing the aircraft in the USA and having the pilots do their training there, Europe's unpredictable weather invariably disrupting and delaying training schedules. There was also the fact that the areas of West Germany over which fast jet training could safely be conducted were very limited. Consequently a decision was taken to transfer all Luftwaffe jet training to America. The first group of 12 pilots arrived in October 1964.

At the very start of the programme, German pilots used American-owned aircraft, but the training agreement stipulated that the Luftwaffe

Below:
Varied markings applied to the first Talons and YF-5s. From left they are: the first production T-38 (58-1194); the prototype YT-38 (58-1191) the third production T-38 (58-1196); the fourth production T-38 (58-1197); the second YT-38 (58-1192); the second production T-38 (58-1195); the second YF-5A (59-4988); and the first YF-5A (59-4987). *Wheeler*

would procure its own aircraft to avoid any compromise of ATC's own programme.

The Federal German Government approved the purchase of the T-38 and T-37 in July 1965 and the Defence Ministry ordered 47 T-37Bs for basic training and 46 T-38As for advanced jet training. The aircraft were financed in fiscal year 1966, the Talons being drawn from a batch of 56 aircraft built as T-38A-65-NOs serialled 66-8349 to 66-8404.

Headquartered at Fort Bliss, the entire Luftwaffe jet training organisation was transferred to the US starting in April 1966. Known as Deutsches Luftwaffen-Ausbildungs-Kommando USA (Dt-LwAusbKdo USA), the Luftwaffe Training Command controlled three squadrons — the 1st at Williams (basic and advanced); the 2nd at Luke (operational training; and the 3rd at Keesler, Mississippi for radar and electronics training.

1.DtLwAusbKdo moved to Sheppard AFB, Texas when the first aircraft were delivered, to come under the 3630th Fighter Training Wing organisation of ATC. The first T-38, *City of Wichita Falls*, arrived in February 1967. The Talons and T-37s at Sheppard were integrated into the inventory of the 3630th FTW and were not used exclusively by German students.

Prospective jet pilots joined 1.DtLwAusbKdo USA for a 53-week course consisting of theoretical instruction combined with 132 hours on the T-37 and 130 hours on the T-38. They then moved to Luke AFB for operational training on the TF/F-104G or returned to Germany to fly the Fiat G-91 with Weapons School 50.

The Luftwaffe training programme went ahead with the routine smoothness that became a hallmark of T-38 operations; attrition was accept-ably low and the first Talon loss did not occur until the summer of 1967, when one exploded shortly after take-off. Even a decade on from the arrival of the first group of German trainees, it was reported that there were still 42 T-38As in service.

Although the changes made to the T-38 throughout its lifetime were not to be extensive, Northrop did develop additional capability for the USAF's foremost trainer by making provision for it to carry weapons. With very limited US procurement of the F-5B and only small numbers of them available to MAP training programmes, it was logical to give the Talon some 'teeth' to enhance the realism of pilot training. The first T-38 to be fitted with a weapons store was 60-576, part of the third production batch. This aircraft was redesignated AT-38, Northrop's 'lead-in fighter'. An elector rack could be attached to the pylon, which was situated under the second cockpit, and was stressed to take the SUU-20A rocket/practice bomb carrier, a practice bomb rack or a minigun pod. Other T-38s were subsequently modified as attack trainers. As T-38Bs in small numbers from various production batches.

Talon production in response incremental buys by the USAF settled down to about 140 per year. As new aircraft were accepted by ATC and the first months saw an accumulation of sorties, the only real drawback of the design was revealed — it had no means of coping with icing conditions: both the airframe and particularly the engines were suceptible to ice damage. All this meant was that flight planning had to take careful account of the conditions that Talons might encounter, particularly during stormy weather and the winter months generally.

The T-38 was fed into the ATC undergraduate

Bottom left:
The first YT-38 showing test equipment filling most of the available space in the second cockpit, the canopy of which is coated over — a feature of the evaluation aircraft in general. *Wheeler*

Above:
Released at the time of the August 1961 order for 144 aircraft, this photograph shows a T-38A-15, part of the second production batch of eight. Liberal areas of day-glo red were applied to all the prototypes, early production T-38s and the YF-5s. *via Mike Hooks*

Right:
Northrop general manager Richard R. Nolan chats to Lt-Col Charles W. Clark as the 100th T-38 is readied for moving from Hawthorne to the company's Palmdale facility in California for final assembly and checking before delivery to the USAF. The 100th aircraft was part of the seventh production batch, funded in 1961. At that time Lt-Col Clark was USAF plant representative at Northrop. *via Robertson*

Below:
A T-38A-30 at Andrews AFB in December 1962.
R. Becker via Dorr

pilot training programme without delay, rapidly replacing the T-33. As the most powerful trainer possessed by the command, the Talon was the link between the completion of basic training and posting to an operational squadron. Each undergraduate pilot received 30 hours basic training on the Cessna T-41, passing to the T-37 for a further 90 hours before embarking on a 120-hour course on the T-38 to gain full pilot proficiency.

The Air Force accepted the 1,000th T-38A (68-8095) on 7 January 1969, by which time ATC was using the aircraft at nine different bases. The 10th to receive Talons was Colombus, Mississippi, the 3650th Pilot Training Wing taking delivery of the first of its assigned 80 aircraft in the spring of that year. A further significant milestone for the T-38 in 1969 was an order for five placed by the US Navy for the Test Pilot School at NATC Patuxent River, Maryland.

ATC's large inventory of T-38s has led to numerous secondments to other USAF commands for a variety of training programmes. In the late

Above:

The first home of the Talon was Williams AFB, Arizona where these FY 1965 machines were photographed. Most of the regular ATC T-38 squadrons identified their aircraft by coloured tail bands, in this case red. Also carried is the ATC badge and the ribbon of the Distinguished Unit Citation.

1970s the Talon even joined SAC, being employed as an economical alternative to training co-pilots to command standard and thus avoiding extra utilisation of the force's ageing B-52 fleet. The T-38s were used by most SAC bomber bases, under the auspices of the 9th SRW, headquartered at Beale AFB, California. The ACE (Accelerated Co-pilot Enrichment) programme usually has six T-38s or T-37s on hand.

One duty from which the T-38 is not expected to return is that of drone work. The US Navy has used the Talon for this duty as the QT-38 for some years, the machines being 'flown' by pilots at the China Lake Naval Weapons Centre.

4 Fighter Trainer

On 25 April 1962 Northrop was informed that the Department of Defense had selected the N-156C for MAP support under Specific Operational Requirement 199. The original FX configuration had provided for only minimum fighter capability and one of the first actions by Northrop was to update the aircraft in compliance with DoD directives. Essentially this exercise included installation of armament and fitting an additional fuel tank in the nose bay. The designation F-5 was allocated on 9 August and the aircraft was officially named Freedom Fighter.

The third N-156C (59-4989) became the third YF-5A and flew on 31 July 1963; it incorporated all GOR 199 requirements including a strengthened wing stressed to carry external loads on four pylons, two wing stations having been added to the fit of the first two prototypes. An initial production contract for 71 aircraft was issued on 22 October, at a fixed price of $20 million. A second for 99 machines was signed on 27 August, USAF F-5 programme funding having been increased to $83 million in June. Each F-5A carried an individual price tag of approximately $600,000, the cost of each aircraft allocated under MAP being borne partially or wholly by the US government depending on arrangements with the country concerned. The first production F-5A (63-8637) flew in October 1963 and Northrop had built eight by the following April.

Early orders were for both single and two-seat versions, it having been decided that pilots who would fly the F-5 operationaly would be better served by the availability of a dual control trainer possessing similar weight, handling and performance characteristics to the fighter. Procurement of the two-seat F-5B was therefore initiated concurrently with the F-5A at a ratio of one of the former to every nine of the latter.

Engineering changes necessary to create the trainer were confined mainly to the fuselage; similar in appearance to the T-38, the F-5B had the same 46ft 4in fuselage with 3in more undercarriage track as on the F-5A (11ft as against 10ft 9in on the T-38) and the longer wheelbase of the Talon. The F-5B also retained the wing leading edge flaps and root extension of the F-5A. There was slight modification to the air intakes for the J85-GE-13 engines of 4,080lb st with afterburning.

The stronger wing enabled the F-5B to take loadings more than twice those of the T-38, and take-off weight was 19,700lb, considerably more than the Talon's 11,700lb. Whereas the single-seater lifted off at 20,100lb, the installation of the second seat (also raised 10in higher than the front one, as on the T-38), instrumentation, elongated canopy and so forth nevertheless kept the trainer within acceptable weight limits. The twin guns and ammunition feed/stowage of the F-5A were removed.

The maiden flight of the first F-5B, serial number 63-8438, took place on 24 February 1964. Considerable flight testing had already been carried out with this aircraft and the second

Right:
Believed to have been taken just after the first flight of the F-5B, this photo shows the crew wearing parachutes, possibly because the ejector seats were not armed for the first flight, on 24 February 1964.

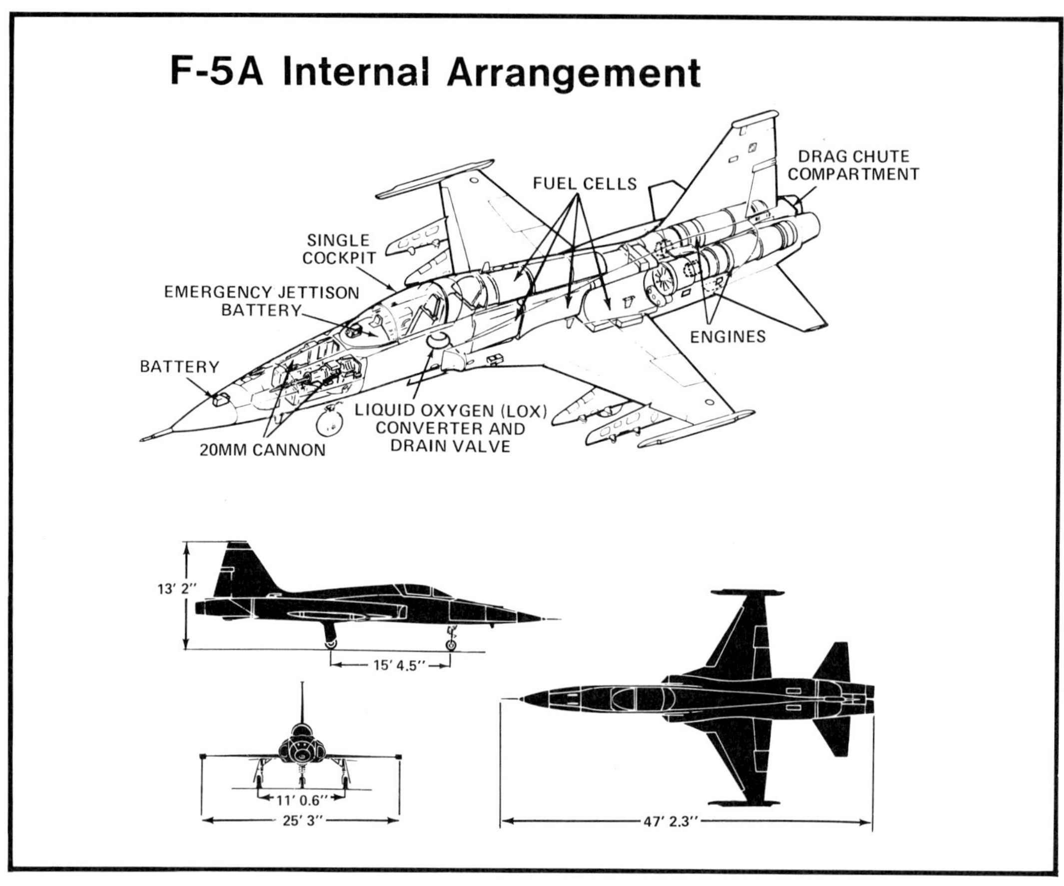

example (63-8439) before 63-8438 went supersonic in a dive on 28 February. The −13 engines gave the F-5B a 'red line' speed of Mach 1.34 as against Mach 1.4 for the F-5A although both early versions of the Freedom Fighter were limited in performance by the power available from engines that had yet to be fully developed.

Production of the F-5B was initiated rapidly and Air Force acceptance took place in March, the aircraft being declared operational on 30 April, four months before the F-5A. On that date World War 2 fighter ace Maj General John C. Meyer officially introduced the F-5B into Tactical Air Command's training programme for personnel of MAP countries. Formal acceptance by Meyer, then Commander of the 12th Air Force, was at Williams AFB, Arizona, which became the main centre for the extensive F-5 conversion courses which were to come. The 4441st Combat Crew Training Squadron welcomed the first foreign pilots that month.

Confirmation that a number of countries had selected the F-5 followed rapidly. In February Norway, having made some adjustments to its defence budget, announced that it would meet just

over a third of the total cost of 64 aircraft (later raised to 68) for delivery in 1966-67.

Northrop completed another five F-5Bs (63-8440 to 63-8444) before selecting the eighth example (63-8445) as a company demonstrator. This aircraft undertook its first sales tour in 1964, visiting 12 European and Middle Eastern countries between 15 June and 15 September. For part of the tour it was based at Evreaux, northwest of Paris, where British journalist John Fricker was able to make a first-hand evaluation of its flight characteristics. John occupied the second seat while Northrop test pilot John Fritz kept an eye on things up front. Selected parts of Fricker's report follow.

The F-5B had taken off from the French base and been flown rather undramatically when John Fritz put it into a vertical climb. At 17,000ft everything went quiet when Fritz closed both throttles. His 'back seater' watched with 'apprehensive fascination the inexorable retreat of the ASI needle towards the zero mark' — whereupon Fritz raised both hands above his head. . .

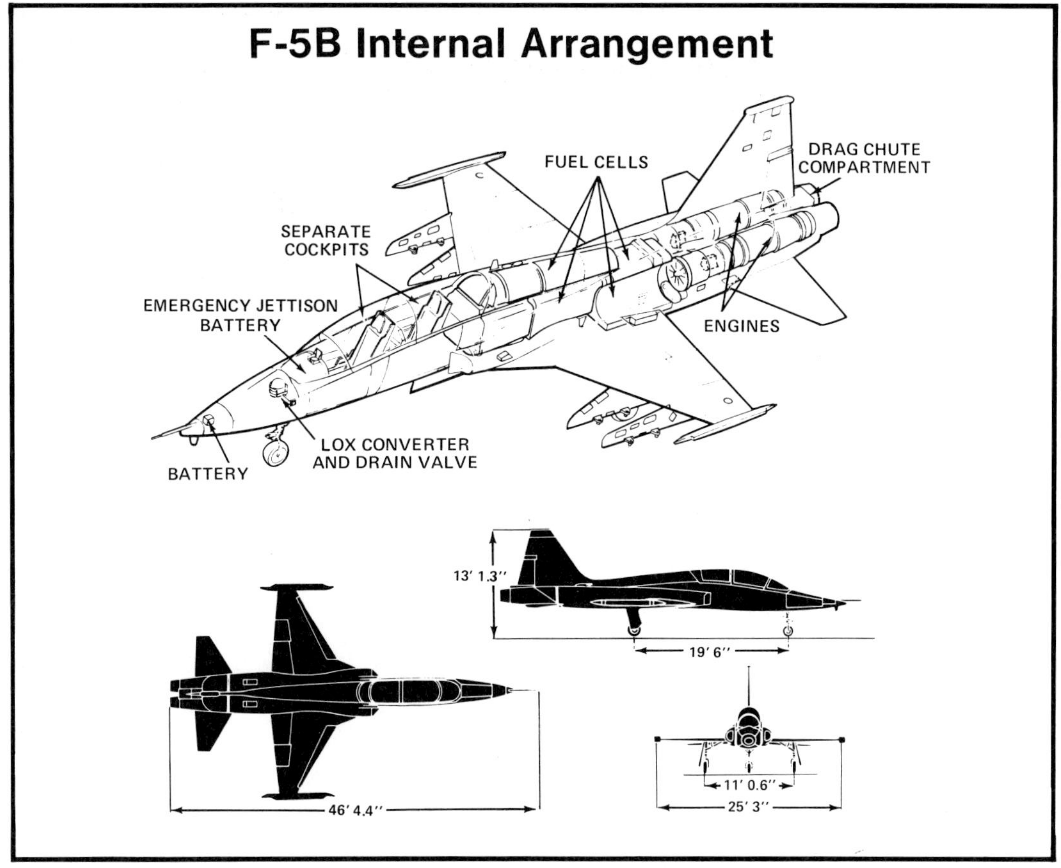

F-5B Internal Arrangement

'This did not seem to me to be the most appropriate time to leave a high-performance fighter entirely to its own devices . . . but the F-5B slowly and majestically began to nose over in a gentle parabola, still hands off, with the wings absolutely level. A brief moment of zero g as we coasted down towards the horizon, and then our mount completed its demonstration of classic docility by diving itself almost as steeply downwards to recover flying speed.'

Earlier, the writer had doubted the F-5B's slow speed handling and opined: 'Here indeed was a typical underwinged hot-rod which would exhibit all the gliding qualities of a streamlined brick at the low end of the speed scale'. As the sortie progressed, Fricker was delighted to be proved wrong. At about 20,000ft he was invited to try a clean stall.

'With the confidence of a Russian roulette player I blipped out the vertical air brakes to reduce speed to about 220kt and carried on easing back the stick, as directed from the front seat, for a 1g stall. As the speed crept back, slight high-frequency airframe buffet started at about 135kt IAS, but just when the bottom should have fallen out of everything, I found that the stick was fully back, and we were mushing down nose high at about 127kt IAS. Lateral control was still available, resulting in typical American lightplane stalling characteristics, suitably scaled-up in airspeed and rate of descent, but almost as innocuous.'

'Clean, the F-5 has a nose-high rate of sink of about 4,000-5,000ft/min at its minimum flight speed, and these values decrease with similar characteristics following undercarriage and flap deflection. Unlike the T-38 the F-5 series had leading-edge wing flaps which operate with the wide-chord trailing-edge flaps for take-off and landing, with full deflection used in each case. Alternatively, the middle setting of the flap lever lowers the leading edge sections only, for combat manoeuvring up to 300kt. Flap and air brake movement are both linked mechanically with the tailplane to cancel out trim changes.

'Without leading edge extension, at medium altitudes, the F-5 can be racked round in tight turns at low airspeeds (about 220kt) into pre-stall buffet without any tendency to flick. Out of the

corner of your eye you can see the slender area-ruled tip tanks nodding in phase with the airframe flexure, but it soon becomes evident that the F-5 is one of the most docile and forgiving of any combat aircraft.'

Commenting on the powerplants, Fricker said:

'Twin engines in a fighter mean low attrition rates, and when the powerplants reach the 7:1 thrust/weight ratios of the J85s in the F-5 they confer similar stores-carrying capabilities to strike fighters a third as large again. As a key to the F-5 concept the J85s are tiny but sophisticated units which are miserly on fuel, and at the moment develop 4,080lb maximum thrust for a weight of only 585lb. In the J85-GE-15, maximum output is increased to 4,300lb for take-off and climb by the provision of additional intake air through controllable plenum chamber doors. In engines of this size, small increments of thrust represent quite large percentage increases, and the 96% duct recovery of the -15 boosts the interception rate of climb from its current 30,000ft/min for example, to 37,000ft/min.

'The J85s in the F-5 have fully variable afterburning with automatic nozzle control. Among the engine instruments are duplicated nozzle position indicators, graduated in percentages of available travel, which provide a check on afterburner operation. In full cold thrust (military power) the nozzles are only about 5% open, but in afterburning, the tailpipe diameter is increased by 60-70% nozzle opening to maintain the jetpipe temperature limit of 650°C. As a safeguard the nozzle will not open until afterburner combustion has been achieved, to avoid a large potential power loss, which can be encountered with such installations in say, the F-104G'.

'Cockpit layout is of striking simplicity, but there is ample elbow-room despite the lightweight concept, except possibly where headroom in the

Top:
The first F-5B takes off on an early test flight, well loaded with drop tanks and Bullpup AGMs. The second cockpit houses test equipment. *Dorr*

Bottom:
Lift off for the second F-5B. By April 1964 the B model was in service at Williams AFB. *Dorr*

Right:
Interesting comparison between the F-5B and T-38, the former being the sixth production aircraft. Note the black anti-glare panels on the B model's tip tanks.

rear cockpit is concerned. Large diameter flight instruments come as a pleasant surprise in the F-5, especially as they conform to the basic airline 'T' layout. Navaids include TACAN, ILS and ADF, with a distance feeder-counter in the central RMI. The single-needle ASI has knots on the outer scale, reading up to 800, with Mach showing in an inset window. Clean, the F-5 has dynamic pressure limits equivalent to Mach 1.72 or 710kt EAS, but its performance falls well short at the moment because of its available power.

'The F-5 is currently just sub-sonic at low level, but with the -15 engines, maximum low altitude speed should increase to Mach 1.04. Controls are fully-powered hydraulically, with duplicated systems and dual or tandem actuators. In keeping with the general simplicity, there is no g-feel or airspeed input, but springs and a bob-weight give graduation of stick-force per g, which reaches a maximum at about Mach 0.9.

'Northrop's control system results in beautifully smooth handling characteristics, with a complete absence of the normal lateral break-out effort and accompanying tendency to over-control. Taking over at 20,000ft in supersonic flight after John Fritz's impressive demonstration of an interception climb, I found that 2g turns could be maintained at Mach 1.2 with full afterburning power, and accurate TACAN headings selected up to 42,000ft.

'The excellence of F-5 control tempts even the tyro jet pilot into emulating an aerobatic ace; rolls are simply a matter of pushing the stick to one side, regardless of which way up you happen to be pointing, and the horizon snaps round obligingly outside the big plastic canopy. Loops require a little more finesse, but with the delicate control available from the slab tailplane I was able to fly the F-5 moderately smoothly on the edge of the buffet boundary round a 4g arc, starting at 450kt taking about 10,000ft of sky, and reaching 150kt on top. During one of the loops, we were inverted with only 130kt on the ASI when John Fritz suggested rolling out. Despite the very low airspeed, a touch of the stick snapped the F-5 right side up very positively.

'The inboard ailerons are sufficiently powerful to achieve a stabilised rate of roll of 400°/sec at Mach 0.8, but consecutive rolling manoeuvres are to be avoided to keep clear of roll coupling instability. As a further safeguard, aileron travel is just about halved automatically when the under-carriage is retracted, and rudder movement was

originally restricted from ±30 to ±6°. For all normal manoeuvres, including aerobatics, this is adequate, but full aileron travel can still be obtained by over-coming a 20lb spring in the circuit. Rudder travel is now being limited by g-forces by making its hydraulic actuators insufficiently powerful to work against high dynamic loads.

'The only clean flight condition likely to require full control travel is a spin, which is difficult to achieve in any of the T-38/F-5 series. The 25° swept wing, which gives the effect of aerodynamic dihedral, results in the usual oscillatory spin of most jets, which normally is accompanied by the flame-out of both engines. Recovery action is similarly standard among jets, and comprises full pro-spin aileron (into the direction of rotation), full opposite rudder, and aft stick. In an inverted spin, according to the book, all controls should be centralised, but if recovery has not been achieved by 10,000ft, the drill is to eject.

'No rudder trim is provided, although the F-5 has the standard actuator thumb button on the stick, with a trim actuator on the panel, for longitudinal adjustment. The J85s, with their automatic fuel control, can put up with any amount of mishandling, and a demonstration 'tiger' air start at 20,000ft, in which the throttle is left in full afterburner, to where the throttle accelerates in its own time of 17 seconds from relighting, was completely painless. The J85s will accelerate from flight idle of 48%rpm to 100% (military) power in 4-6 seconds, and with afterburners in, aircraft acceleration is corre-

spondingly brisk from low airspeeds. The F-5 has insufficient power margin at the moment to go supersonic in dry (cold) thrust, and at high altitudes takes about 2½ minutes to accelerate from Mach 0.9 to 1.3 with full afterburning in level flight. Supersonic runs are therefore normally achieved by diving, to save fuel, and the F-5 is unable to exceed Mach 1 with external stores.'

John Fricker and John Fritz finished their flight with an attack profile and a little combat manoeuvring:

' . . . at a conservative 259kt on a typical target search. A steep turn at 95% rpm into buffet was smoothed out by extending the leading edge flap, and 2g and 230kt, then maintaining a vertical pivot of lightplane radius around the quivering wingtip tank. 'And now' came the voice from the front seat, 'we want to make a pass at the target.' A spine-jarring punch from the afterburners, and we slammed into a vicious 4g turn on the black-out threshold at 350kt, to skim back over the pre-selected point just above the trees just 35 seconds later.

'Armament trials have shown that the F-5 is an excellent weapons platform, but as a measure of defensive capability, we completed the sortie by an evasive 4g spiral afterburner climb. In this sustained graunching turn, the F-5B accelerated from 300kt, gained altitude and g-turned simultaneously to make a very difficult target. After a single-engined touch and go we completed our 50-minute sortie with 600lb of fuel remaining, by a full-stop arrival on the squashy 11ft/sec soft-field undercarriage, turning off at the first intersection after a ground run of less than 2,000ft. Our 15ft tail parachute seemed to stop us almost instantly, from a 155kt approach, and provides sufficient drag to prevent taxying until jettisoned.'

Below:
The eighth production F-5B became a much travelled company demonstrator — as evidenced by the national flags of customer countries on the nose. The fuselage/fin stripe was blue. *Dorr*

5 Global Defender

The First Foreign Tigers

On 1 February 1965 the Imperial Iranian Air Force became the first foreign recipient of the F-5A when 13 aircraft (11 F-5As and two F-5Bs) of an initial batch arrived at the 1st Fighter Air Base at Mehrabad, to re-equip squadrons previously flying F-84 Thunderjets in the strike role. This purchase marked the start of a phenomenal build-up in Iran's military airpower over the next 14 years or so and the country became a primary customer for a number of leading US aerospace companies.

The IIAF F-5s became operational in June 1965, by which time the first squadron was at full strength with a second in the process of converting, the order book having then reached 91 aircraft. In March that year the F-5 had completed a series of flight tests under different climatic conditions. The tests lasted seven months and gave Northrop valuable information on the widely differing conditions the F-5 was about to meet, as early customer deliveries commenced to nations in Europe and the Middle and Far East.

Delivery of the F-5 to the IIAF was the end of the first phase of the MAP training programme for the new type, the first 'class' of foreign pilots having assembled at Williams AFB in September 1964. It included six Iranian pilots, four Koreans and two Americans from the USAF's Military Assistance Advisory Group (MAAG). MAAG played an extremely important part in the MAP,

its personnel working closely with each different air arm in order to integrate the Freedom Fighter into inventory in the most cost-effective way. Teams were placed in each country to initiate national training programmes and generally assist in getting new American aircraft into service as smoothly and as quickly as possible.

Each MAP pilot received some 40 hours' flight training at Williams, preceded by an English language course where necessary, along with 115 hours of classroom instruction and 50 hours of 'briefing and critiques'. The 4441st had at the start of the MAP training programme, seven F-5As and five F-5Bs. Pilots flew about 15 hours instruction in the two-seaters and 25 hours in the F-5A, the curriculum covering formation flying, instrument flying, air-to-air and air-to-ground gunnery, missile attack profiles and air combat manoeuvring.

Along with pilots, Williams' instructors trained 50 men in ground trades, passing on their expertise in the whole range of aircraft support and maintenance skills. These courses varied from 85 hours to 250, depending on the complexity of the

Below:
The first examples of the F-5A for the Imperial Iranian Air Force, the type's initial customer. Some of these long-serving machines later served other countries when Iran modernised with the F-5E. *Wheeler*

subject, and were ably assisted by F-5 simulators and associated training aids.

The 4441st quickly achieved a high state of readiness and utilisation on the F-5 in the first few months of operation at Williams, averaging out at about 80%. Flying time of 25 hours per month per aircraft, a rate which had been established as the ideal beforehand, was achieved and maintained. Target maintenance hours per flying hour, set at 21, settled down to about 23 hours early in the programme.

Having completed the course in Arizona, Iranian pilots returned home and proceeded to convert their squadron colleagues after a short refresher flying course. Assisted by a USAF Mobile Training Team (MTT), the Iranians then checked out in combat training — gunnery, tactics, bombing and missile attack using the ubiquitous AIM-9 Sidewinder in its B configuration. Quantities of Sidewinders and other weapons were supplied under MAP along with the F-5; Iran was among the countries which also received the Northrop SUU-20 combined bomb and rocket dispenser, a useful and economical training aid carried on the fuselage pylon of the F-5. Also used was the 2.75in FFAR and a range of unguided bombs.

MTTs were usually established in each country about three months before the arrival of aircraft and worked with MAAG personnel and local mililtary organisations to ensure that there was the minimum of delay in getting the new aircraft operational. In Iran the F-5 operational ready rate quickly reached 80%.

A slightly lower rate of about 70% was achieved by the South Koreans for their F-5s, the first of which arrived early in April 1965. Twenty aircraft (16 F-5As and four F-5Bs) were used to re-equip the 105th Fighter Squadron of the 10th FW at Suwon, which achieved combat status on 1 Sep-

tember. In the meantime another 14 F-5As were delivered for the 102nd FS also at Suwon. As with the IIAF, the ROKAF's aircraft utilisation rate was initially set at 13 flying hours per aircraft per month. This was rapidly reached due in no small part to the F-5's excellent serviceability record, enabling the type to become an integral part of mission planning in a remarkably short time. In Korea's case the slightly lower ready rate then achieved by Iran was apparently because of a temporary shortage of spares.

Early orders for South Korea totalled 87 F-5As and 35 F-5Bs, the ROKAF becoming one of the largest users of the type. An aerobatic team, the 'Black Eagles', was one of several formed on the F-5A in various parts of the world, the Koreans also utilising the RF-5A for some shows. At least 10 RF-5As were delivered to equip a single squadron, this unit remaining with the RF-5A some time after the early fighter/trainer models had been replaced by the F-5E and F-5F. And by the late 1970s, Korea was undertaking local assembly of Tigers — the Hanjin Corporation, a subsidiary of Korean Air Lines, carrying out this work using components supplied by Northrop. Extensive overhaul and maintenance facilities were also established, enabling the Koreans to become virtually self-sufficient in maintaining one of their air force's most important aircraft.

Below:
South Korea was to maintain one of the world's largest inventories of F-5s subsequent to the first F-5A and B deliveries in 1965. The 105th FS, 10th FW at Suwon received the aircraft pictured here on 30 April that year.
via Dorr

Top right:
Also part of the 105th FS in 1965, this particular F-5A was one of 31 passed to South Vietnam in the early 1970s.
via Dorr

Hellenic Tigers

Greece received initial examples of the F-5 in the same month as Norway, June 1965. At that time Greece was a full member of NATO with its air force forming part of the 6th Allied Tactical Air Force, and 80 aircraft (55 F-5As, 16 RF-5As and nine F-5Bs) were ordered under MAP to equip two *pterighe* (wings) in the 28th Tactical Air Command.

The first *Mira* (squadron) to equip was 341 at Néa Ankhialos in 111 Wing which became operational on 15 July with 15 F-5As. The following year 343 *Mira* (113 Wing) had converted at Thessaloniki-Mikra but a planned third (III Wing) squadron, 349 *Mira*, was only partially equipped when deteriorating relations with the US resulted in an arms embargo being imposed on Greece. This resulted in an order shortfall of 30 F-5s pending an improvement on the political front.

This improvement occurred late in 1968, when deliveries resumed; the Greeks completed the re-equipment of 349 *Mira*, eventually receiving a total of 114 F-5As, including four ex-Iranian machines (passed on when Iran bought the F-5E), 34 RF-5As and 20 F-5Bs. All the RF-5As were apparently used by 349 *Mira*, otherwise all three squadrons had a mix of A and B models. The early model F-5s were destined for two decades of service with the Greek Air Force, many of the original aircraft remaining in service today. Attrition rate has generally been acceptable although at least nine F-5As and one reconnaissance model have been written off.

Tigers Over The Fjords

As related earlier, Norway was able to part-finance supplies of F-5s under MAP by reducing the planned number of F-104 Starfighter squadrons in inventory from two to one. The first aircraft for the RNorAF flew on 17 June 1965 and was delivered to No 336 Squadron at Rygge after a 6,200-mile transit flight from Edwards. One of the original three ferry pilots said of the aircraft, 'They climb like homesick angels'. The Norwegian aircraft were initially known as F-5A (G)s in Northrop

Below:
Sporting the distinctive black and blue axehead of No 332 Squadron Royal Norwegian AF, this F-5B also has the RAF-style code letters in use since World War 2.
Jerry Geer via Dorr

Top:
In natural aluminium, rather than the subsequently introduced overall grey, F-5A 67-14904 was the second to last delivered to the RNorAF. Its coding denotes No 336 Squadron at Rygge. *Geer via Dorr*

Above:
No 334 Squadron at Bodo also, it appears, had a plentiful supply of camouflaged drop tanks for its F-5As. *Geer via Dorr*

records, although this designation was subsequently dropped.

Norwegian aircraft had JATO provision, windscreen de-icing and arrester hooks, all of which increased operational efficiency of aircraft obliged to operate from less than hospitable airfields. Between 1966 and 1968 Norway received 56 F-5As and 24 F-5Bs, these machines equipping Nos 336 (Rygge), 338 (Orland), 332 (Rygge), and 334 (Bodo). Each squadron had a statutory strength of 20 aircraft, assigned to Allied Forces Northern Europe.

The Norwegians were to suffer an abnormally high attrition rate with the F-5, 16 aircraft being written off by the mid-1970s. The loss of these F-5As plus one F-5B forced some redeployment of strength and by 1974 the survivors were distributed among three strike squadrons, No 332 being disbanded in 1972. This left No 336 as the only F-5 unit at Rygge. Having received its first aircraft in March 1966, No 336 pioneered the F-5's entry to Norwegian service and in 1979 celebrated its 30th anniversary, having started operations from Gardermoen on 1 July 1949.

At the celebrations held to mark this occasion, squadron commander Maj Einar Smedsvig said that his squadron had flown the F-5 'Around the world 1,000 times'. He had then completed 1,000 hours on the F-5A and B, while Capt Nordby had 2,500 hours and Capt Aas 2,000 hours. The RNorAF achieved its 1,000th flight with the F-5 in May 1979.

Right:
CF-5D No 116801 of the Aerospace Evaluation & Test Establishment operating from CFB Cold Lake. These CF-5s are mainly used for photo chase, supplementing CT-133 Silver Stars. The unit operates three examples of the type, two Ds and an A. *Peter Foster*

Photographed a few months after delivery in 1965, the Turkish Air Force's F-5As equipped units in the 1st and 3rd Tactical Air Forces.

Turkish Delight

With an inventory of predominantly US-designed aircraft since the end of World War 2, the Turk Hava Kuvvetleri began a modernisation programme in the early 1960s in order to maintain its commitment to NATO and offer some significant defence for its border regions abutting Eastern bloc territories. The THK's 1st and 3rd Tactical Air Forces were assigned entirely to NATO and both maintained some strike capability as well as that of air defence. Northrop F-5As were used to modernise squadrons composed of ageing F-84 Thunderjets and Thundersteaks, the first examples being received early in 1966.

Two squadrons of 18 F-5As were formed initially, based at Bandirma and Balikesir, each with a primary air defence commitment and a secondary close support role. Turkey's allocation of F-5s was 140 aircraft although it was US policy in the 1960s to supply these on a gradual basis. Consequently re-equipment of the F-84 units took some years and although there were four squadrons of F-5s in service by the early 1970s, the old Republic fighter-bombers configured both for ground attack and reconnaissance, were still much in evidence.

Licence-Built In Spain

Northrop's part stake in the Spanish aerospace concern Constucciones Aeronauticas S.A. (CASA) led to agreement on licence assembly when the Spanish Air Force decided to modernise its fighter attack element with the F-5A in 1966. A

Bottom left:
The first eight SF-5Bs (CE-9s) assembled in Spain from Northrop supplied components, outside the CASA plant at Seville in June 1968. *via Dorr*

Above:
It is common for aerospace companies to paint aircraft in customer's markings for publicity photographs, although these invariably show some discrepancies. It is even easier to retouch a photograph, this being one of the SF-5As for the Spanish AF — known as C.9s rather than C.7s. No production machine had this serial. *via Dorr*

total of 70 machines was covered by the order: 19 F-5As, 34 F-5Bs and 17 RF-5A. These took the dual designations SF-5A, SF-5B and (initially) SRF-5A to distinguish them from US-built aircraft, and the Spaniards, in common with other aircraft in inventory, applied their own set of designators, these being respectively C.9, CE.9 and CR.9, the F-5 being the ninth fighter type operated since the Ejercito del Aire became an independent service in July 1939.

The first eight complete aircraft were supplied by Northrop and thereafter CASA's plants at Seville and Madrid-Getafe assembled the balance of 62 from components shipped from the US, the first example being rolled out in June 1968 at Madrid. The construction programme lasted until 1971.

Entering service with Escuadrones 202, 204, 211 and 212, the CASA F-5s were for some years the primary Spanish air defence ground attack fighter, but a reorganisation programme which took effect in December 1976 brought a degree of unit reassignment. Esc 202 and 204 became respectively 731 and 732 of the Escuela de Reactores, and Esc 211 and 212 were grouped under Ala (Interceptor Wing) 21. Esc 212 then

became Esc 464 under Ala 46, whereupon the F-5s took their current designations of A.9, AE.9 and AR.9.

Operational attrition up to the spring of 1982 claimed one A.9, four AE.9s and two AR.9s, none of which is believed to have been replaced, leaving an inventory of 18 single seaters, 30 trainers and 15 reconnaissance models. Distribution among the four units is as follows: Esc 211 has aircraft of all three sub-types at Moron for fighter ground attack, reconnaissance and training; Esc 464 a similar mix of aircraft at Las Palmas; while Esc 731 and 732 at Talavera la Real support a training force of AE.9s.

Freedom Fighters of the World
Nationalist China (Taiwan) declared its first F-5A squadron operational as part of the 1st Tactical Fighter Wing on 9 December 1965. These early aircraft were procured under both MAP and FMS

Overleaf:

Top left:
Swiss Flugwaffe J-3011 (ex-76-1536) landing at Dubendorf in August 1979. *Peter Foster*

Bottom left:
CF-5A No 116720 of No 433 Squadron landing at CFB Bagotville, which the unit shares with its sister squadron, No 434. *Peter Foster*

Top right:
This fine view of the F-20 Tigershark makes obvious the aircraft's ancestry.

Bottom right:
A pair of F-5Es of the 57th TFTW at Nellis AFB Nevada take off for another sortie in their Aggressor training programme of dissimilar air combat manoeuvring. *Mike Hooks*

F-20
F-20 Tigershark

USAF
01512
AIR FORCE
12
USAF
01531
U.S. AIR FORCE
31

arrangements and well over 100 including F-5Bs were eventually delivered to re-equip two wings of F-86 Sabres. This sizeable inventory allowed China to transfer 48 F-5As to South Vietnam before the end of the war, by which time licence production of the F-5E had started. The inventory of early models remained more or less stable after 1973, two first-line squadrons operating a combined total of 42 F-5As and 10 F-5Bs and two Air Reserve Force squadrons operating about 30. Other F-5s equip a combat crew training centre which now converts pilots to the F-5E, while final phase jet pilot training is on the remaining T-38As, 30 of which were obtained under MAP.

In 1967 Chile was among the South American countries which expressed interest in the F-5A, but the prevailing US arms embargo prevented any procurement until 1973, by which time the F-5E was made available.

Ethiopia obtained enough F-5As to equip one squadron in 1967, this being based at Havar Meda. At least 12 A models and two F-5Bs were delivered by the US under MAP but supplies were suspended in 1975 after a Marxist government was elected. Attrition was meanwhile made good by ex-Iranian aircraft on an ad hoc basis and MAP deliveries resumed briefly in 1977, but with Ethiopia becoming increasingly within the sphere of influence of the USSR, the country's inventory

of Western aircraft gradually gave way to Soviet types. US MAAG personnel were expelled in 1977 and the war with Somalia began before the end of that year.

North Vietnam offered to supply spares from its captured stocks of ex-SVNAF aircraft and the Ethiopians managed to maintain their single F-5 squadron with a mix of A and E models. In the early 1980s this unit was reportedly based at Asmara-Yoannes IV, within range of the Somalian border, and F-5s have almost certainly flown combat missions during the conflict; two F-5As were reported to have flown to the Sudan, where their pilots sought political asylum.

Although eight F-5As and two F-5Bs were acquired by Libya before the military coup of 1969 — when US assistance ceased — they are believed to have been used only briefly. The country lacks adequate numbers of skilled personnel and relies heavily on other countries for aircraft support. Strained diplomatic relations between the USA and Col Gadhafi's Islamic-based revolutionary state resulted in no spares supply or support — in 1975 Northrop said publicly that it had 'no idea how the Libyan F-5s were supported'.

Some sources state that Libya obtained the services of some Greek Air Force personnel — and Pakistan may well have assisted after Libya 'loaned' it F-5s during the 1971 war with India.

These aircraft apparently were used only for training by the PAF, possibly with a view to acquiring F-5s in the future. A decade or more on shows this to be unlikely, however.

Morocco was an early customer for the F-5A and its pilots were represented at Williams from the first days of the MAP training courses for the type. An initial order for 18 F-5As and two F-5Bs was fulfilled in 1967 and subsequent inventory reached 23 fighters and two trainers, attrition being made good by a small number transferred by Iran, including two RF-5As. These aircraft equipped two squadrons of the Royal Moroccan AF at Kenitra on the Atlantic coast.

Still maintaining patrols of the disputed Western Sahara area, Morocco is financially unable to build a large inventory of combat aircraft, but subsequently acquired F-5Es (after twice rejecting US offers of the type) paid for by Saudi Arabia.

Jordan acquired F-5As to replace Hawker Hunter F73As and Bs which were themselves replacements for the entire first-line Hunter force destroyed during the June 1967 Six Day War with Israel. The Freedom Fighter consequently became — with F-104 interceptors — the principal combat type of the Royal Jordanian Air Force into the 1970s when 30 ex-IIAF aircraft were transferred by Iran with US blessing.

Above left:
A fighter patrol by Chinese Nationalist F-5As in the mid-1960s. Of this quartet, '325 was passed to Vietnam and '326 and 328 were subsequently written off in Taiwan. *via Dorr*

Below:
The Philippine Air Force formed its Blue Diamonds aerobatic team on the F-5A, an early delivery batch example being seen here. The team was formed by the only Philippine Air Force Freedom Fighter unit, the 6th TFS at Basa. *Wheeler*

Overleaf:
Royal Jordanian F-5Es were visitors to IAT 1981 at Greenham Common. *Peter March*

Inset, left:
F-5A-20 64-13314 of the 23rd TFW, SVNAF. Judging from its weathered appearance, this photo was taken after many missions had been flown. *Dave Menard*

Inset, right:
Philippine Air Force F-5A-30 (66-9148) at Clark Air Base with 64-13324, an F-5A-20, behind. Both aircraft were operated by the 6th TFS, different tail markings presumably being to differentiate flights.

As well as F-5As, the RJAF acquired four F-5Bs from Iran, these aircraft equipping Nos 1 and 5 Squadrons, the two units sharing Mafraq-King Hussain AB. They were primarily ground support and interception squadrons, using the F-5A for visual air-to-ground operations using VORTAC (combined VOR/TACAN information from a single ground station) and a fixed sighting system. No 5 Squadron also functioned as an operational conversion unit for the F-5A.

The first F-5A for the Philippine Air Force was accepted on 25 October 1966, the aircraft partially replacing the F-86 Sabre in the interceptor role with the 6th Tactical Fighter Squadron in the 5th FW based at Basa on Luzon. A total of 19 A models and three F-5Bs were acquired, and the 6th TFS also supports the air force aerobatic team, the 'Blue Diamonds'.

With close ties with the USA as a SEATO signatory, Thailand was the second country in South East Asia to fly the F-5A after Vietnam — although the first aircraft arrived before the SVNAF had declared its first squadron operational, in April 1966. The F-5A was used to re-equip No 13 Squadron in the 1st FW flying the

Top:
A standard aircraft of the 6th TFS, Philippine Air Force.
via Dorr

Above:
One of Thailand's early F-5 deliveries was this B model, 63-8439. *Wheeler*

F-86 Sabre from Don Muang. Ultimately 24 F-5As, four RF-5As and three F-5Bs were acquired.

By the early 1980s attrition had whittled the numbers to 12 A models and two F-5Bs and reorganisation of the Thai Air Force following the end of the Vietnam war saw the old RAF-style squadron numbering system give way to a US-patterned wing structure with up to four component squadrons. F-5As remained in the 1st Wing, but with first-line combat aircraft being replaced by a transport wing at Don Muang, the F-5A/RF-5A unit became the 103rd Squadron and moved to the old USAF base at Korat — or Nakhom Ratchasima as it is currently known. (RTAF renumbering consisted of inserting a 'O' between the existing two digits of each unit's number — ie No 13 Squadron became the 103rd Squadron and so forth.)

The Yemen Arab Republic Air Force operates an equal mix of Soviet and Western types, and F-5s equipped a single fighter squadron, 12 F-5Es and four F-5Bs being operated in the early 1980s. Recent reports suggest however that North Yemen's Tigers have been put up for sale, possibly in the interests of standardisation on the MiG-21 as the sole interceptor type, with the Su-23 taking over the secondary F-5B attack role. The F-5 squadron was based at the capital, San'a.

The longevity of the F-5A continues into mid-1980s, not only with existing operators but new ones which are not in a position to afford the latest in aviation hardware. The most recent of these at time of writing was Honduras, which replaced its ancient F-86E Sabres with F-5As in 1985. These machines are believed to be second-hand examples previously operated by Ethiopia and put on the market some years previously. The Freedom Fighters are presumably based at San Pedro Sula and used in the interceptor role.

6 Little Tiger

The first F-5As purchased directly for USAF use were 12 machines, five from FY 1963 and seven from FY 1964 production batches, issued to the 4503rd Tactical Fighter Squadron at Williams, specifically for operational evaluation in South East Asia. Accompanying the squadron personnel to Vietnam was a USAF evaluating team whose job it was to 'obtain information to be used in developing tactical air concepts, procedures, tactics and techniques for the employment of these fighters in combat'. For the F-5 the deployment was a more or less routine continuation of Phase III testing but with the hoped-for advantage of positive results from operating the aircraft under war conditions. Northrop also knew that good reports from the evaluation might influence the Department of Defense in considering a sizeable number of F-5s for Tactical Air Command; the command had in 1965 requested approximately 200 aircraft and the Air Force had also requested the combat evaluation. DoD approval for this was confirmed in July that year.

It took about three months to complete pilot training and combat indoctrination while Northrop modified the dozen F-5As. These, given the temporary designation 'F-5C' (the F-5C was named Tiger I shortly after the USAF deployment began) to distinguish them from standard MAP aircraft, were F-5A-15s and -20s with some modifications to instruments and flight controls,

90kg of belly armour and full provision for in-flight refuelling. The avionics fit was updated and stores pylons were made to jettison in the event of emergency. These aircraft were also the first F-5s to be camouflaged, in the Asia Minor scheme widely adopted for the majority of US combat aircraft operating in the theatre.

Under the name Project 'Skoshi Tiger' ('skoshi' being the Japanese word meaning little) the 4503rd initiated an intensive training programme before leaving the USA. Of primary importance was the need to perfect air-to-air refuelling and to this end pilots practised single and multiple transfers from KC-135 tankers. On 20 October 1965 the small unit left Williams AFB, destination Bien Hoa, South Vietnam. The force routed via Hickam, Hawaii and Anderson AB, Guam and was accompanied across the Pacific by the tankers, arriving at their South Vietnamese base at noon on 23 October. Banners and photographers greeted the F-5s as they taxied into allocated revetments at the busy base. The aircraft were refuelled and that afternoon the F-5 flew its first combat mission.

The following months saw the F-5C integrated into the wide range of operations then being flown in support of the South Vietnamese Army in its operations against the Viet Cong. The year was the final period of the 'advisory' phase for the Americans in SE Asia and the start of a gradual, massive build up of arms and fighting men. The Vietnamese watched the development of F-5 operations with particular interest, for this was the aircraft which it was hoped would give much-needed muscle to their own air force, then equipped solely with obsolescent piston-engined types. The Vietnamese had for some time been

Overleaf:

Left:
Part of the first production batch of F-5As, 63-8381 was flight tested in USAF markings prior to allocation to MAP. It is seen here carrying three napalm tanks and 750lb bombs. *M. Hooks*

Right:
F-5A 64-13332 of the 4503rd TFS at Bien Hoa in December 1965. *Dave Menard*

U.S. AIR FORCE
RESCUE
38381

Top left:
This port side close-up of '428 shows the refuelling probe and other salient details. *Menard*

Top right:
F-5A 63-8429 at Bien Hoa, with napalm tanks on the outer pylons and 250lb bombs inboard. *Menard*

Above:
F-5A-20 63-8428 *Exterminator* in its revetment at Bien Hoa, Vietnam during its service with the 4503rd TFS. *Dave Menard*

urging the supply of jet equipment by their American allies, pointing out with considerable justification that other Asian air forces — which were not fighting a war — had far more modern aircraft.

With the implementation of air strikes by US aircraft prominently marked with national insignia, the nature of the war changed; along with B-57s, F-100s and older types, the F-5Cs flew close support, interdiction, armed recce and escort missions using a variety of ordnance. Ground-fire

suppression sorties were mounted for 'Ranch Hand' defoliation flights and on occasion strikes into North Vietnam would have Tigers along as the MiGCAP, although no contact with enemy fighters was reported during this early phase. For the longer range missions out of Bien Hoa to North Vietnam and Laos the Tigers were air-refuelled.

For MiGCAPs the F-5's wingtip fuel tanks were replaced by AIM-9 Sidewinders but the majority of ground attack missions were flown with the tanks in place and a variety of air-to-ground weapons carried under the wings. Combat loads averaged from 2,300 to 3,000lb, the range of the F-5 so configured being up to 180 nautical miles unrefuelled.

While the reliability of the F-5 under South East Asian combat conditions was generally very good, the evaluation also highlighted some problem areas. It was found for example that 750lb napalm tanks occasionally failed to drop 'clean' from the outboard wing pylons and hit the underside of the wing. The guns were the source of some trouble in that they tended to 'smoke up' the windscreen during firing runs particularly in rainy conditions. Actual windscreen damage was caused by rounds

bursting just ahead of the nose, and gun gases sometimes resulted in engine damage.

These malfunctions were solved by USAF ground crews and Northrop representatives, both 'in theatre' and back at Hawthorne, and the F-5's in commission rate settled down to an admirable average of 96% on any given day, with an abort rate of less than 1% per month. Utilisation rate was 62.5 hours per aircraft per month, with up to 33 sorties being flown daily by the 12 fighters. This effort required 11.9 man hours of maintenance per flying hour in the early period of the test programme and this dropped to 6.5 hours subsequently — far better than the 21 hours predicted by Northrop prior to the deployment. The F-5C consequently achieved the lowest maintenance time per flight hour of any aircraft in the theatre, and the 4503rd's ground support team claimed an engine change record when they removed a J85 from one F-5, replaced it with another and flight-tested the aircraft, all in the space of one hour 50 minutes 'under field conditions'.

Its low fuel burn engines gave the F-5 a useful loiter time on ground support missions, although bomb aiming aids were unsophisticated. A typical mission profile worked out during early tests with the F-5A in the US found that the F-5 could, with

two 50gal tip tanks, three 150gal pylon tanks and two 750ft bombs, operate at a combat radius of approximately 140nm, flying to the target at 5,000ft at a speed of Mach 0.5. At that weight and speed the aircraft could remain in the target area for over an hour and still employ a useful climb at full military power to reach 40,000ft, levelling off for the return flight at Mach 0.84.

Bomb and napalm delivery in Vietnam was (again, typically) from a shallow dive, the pilot judging range using the lead computing gunsight. This was an improvement on the sighting system of earlier F-5As, which had the Norsight fixed optical sight providing basic 10° downwards deflection on air-to-ground attacks, weapons release being (depending on type) effected via a switch panel on the left side of the instrument panel.

Although capable of carrying a large variety of stores, the F-5Cs in Vietnam — along with other USAF ground attack aircraft — rarely carried anything more sophisticated than unguided bombs, napalm and FFAR rocket pods. Range considerations usually dictated at least a 150gal tank on the centreline pylon, boosted if necessary by a pair of 150gal tanks on each inboard wing pylon.

While the USAF's 'Skoshi Tiger' continued its contribution to the Vietnam fighting, the urgent requests for jet aircraft by the Vietnamese Air Force were being met by the US. By the late summer of 1965 the Vietnamese had flown their first jet sorties in B-57s and early in 1966, the Air Force Advisory Group, looking into future needs of its ally, recommended to the DoD that the F-5 be supplied. This was accepted by Secretary of Defense Robert McNamara and in August 32 Vietnamese left for Williams AFB to commence F-5 conversion training.

The first crews returned home to Vietnam in December and established an F-5 pilot conversion programme at Bien Hoa. In January 10 USAF non-commissioned officers and a Northrop-appointed contract engineer also arrived in

Top:
Consecutive Tigers off the line — 64-13317 and 64-13318 in their revments at Bien Hoa in 1966. *Besecker via Dorr*

Above:
A South Vietnamese ground technician prepares to service an F-5A's 20mm guns, taking advantage of the excellent access afforded via the quick-release panels. The aircraft is 64-13314 of the 23rd Wing.
Pacific Stars and Stripes

Vietnam to assist the training and by 10 May 1967, 27 pilots were deemed ready to fly the F-5.

The Vietnamese unit chosen to be the first to operate a jet fighter was the 23rd Wing's 522nd FS, previously flying A-1 Skyraiders. It had been decided that the remaining F-5Cs belonging to the old 5403rd would be passed to the SVNAF as initial equipment, pending the arrival of further aircraft in the country. A nucleus of the 'Skoshi Tiger' pilots then formed the 10th Fighter Commando Squadron early in 1966. The 10th TCS remained at Bien Hoa, one of seven bases in South Vietnam capable of supporting tactical fighter operations at that time, and formed a wing with five squadrons of F-100s: these were the 90th, 308th, 416th, 510th and 531st.

Between October 1965 and March 1966, the

49

5403rd had thoroughly evaluated the F-5 under the most taxing of combat conditions: it had flown 2,659 sorties and logged over 2,500 flying hours during the period. It had been the USAF's intention to deploy two more F-5 squadrons to Vietnam, but this did not occur. Instead, the 10th FCS was boosted in strength by 24 aircraft, new machines taken from MAP production and having similar modifications to those aircraft already in SE Asia. Of the original 12 aircraft, five had been lost by November 1966. Four were shot down (63-8425 being the first) by ground fire and a fifth crashed on take-off because of engine failure.

In order to build up flight hours, the Vietnamese undertook numerous training sorties with their new Tigers, the first examples of which were made available to them in April 1967. Air Marshal Nguyen Coa Ky took a keen personal interest in his prestigious jet fighters, of which the SVNAF was understandably proud. Ky himself checked out in an F-5B soon after the 522nd FS was activated as an F-5 squadron, on 17 April, one Major Sho making the first flight by the unit on the 18th. Squadron Commander Lt-Col Duong Thieu Hung had 17 F-5Cs and two F-5Bs in inventory at the date of the formal ceremony to mark the F-5's operational debut with the SNVAF, an event combined with an open day at Bien Hoa on 1 June.

The remaining 10th FCS F-5s were also handed over to their new owners on 1 June, the occasion being a good excuse to stage a flypast by the 522nd. This was only slightly marred by one F-5 failing to take-off, and thereafter the SVNAF began an intensive period of operations with the black and yellow checkboard-marked F-5s of the 23rd Wing which also included the 514th and 518th Squadrons with A-1s. Observers were impressed by the speed with which the Vietnamese had worked up to operational readiness; the intensive flying rate inevitably caused some lowering of commission rates, albeit temporarily. Several F-5s sustained minor damage when landing at Bien Hoa and an entire year's supply of mainwheel brakes was used up in just one month. The kind of wear and tear under rugged operational conditions was naturally of great interest to Northrop and to glean as much data as possible, the company shipped F-5A-15 64-13317 back to the States. On arrival it was subject to a thorough 'tear down' examination.

The South Vietnamese Air Force fed the F-5 into the daily pattern of operations against Viet Cong and NVA regulars infiltrating the south, although the lion's share of the SVNAF's ground attack operations was still shouldered by the venerable A-1 Skyraider — which was entirely understandable as the F-5 was not available in great numbers. It did however have one great advantage over the old A-1 — speed. While there is no recorded instance of a SVNAF F-5 actually intercepting an enemy aircraft, there were plenty of occasions when pilots were profoundly grateful to streak away from a target area at maximum speed — supersonically if necessary. Ground attack operations within the borders of South Vietnam faced increasingly heavy return fire and while this was nowhere near the scale US aircraft met over the North, the enemy made good use of slim resources using his small arms and machine guns to maximum effect. Unfortunately the pilots flying over the South would soon be on the receiving end of the lethal weapons continually being supplied to North Vietnam by the Russians and the Chinese.

Although the integration of the F-5 into the SVNAF had been smooth enough — and had paved the way for a similar training programme for the Cessna A-37 — the 522nd remained the sole Tiger squadron for about five years. Its efforts were always overshadowed by the huge sortie rate achieved by US air forces although the 1968 Tet offensive gave impetus to the Vietnamese shouldering more responsibility for their protracted, frustrating and seemingly unwinnable conflict. Under plans for 'Vietnamisation' of the war, the US planned to build up South Vietnamese armed forces to an unprecedented level concurrent with withdrawal of its own forces.

As the SVNAF's premier combat aircraft, the F-5 was to figure significantly in this build-up and, critical though they sometimes were of the abilities of their erstwhile allies, the Americans had little choice politically — if not militarily — to press Vietnamisation through with all speed. Thus was seen a complete reversal of US policy — in 1965 there was a marked reluctance to allow the Vietnamese to fly their own jet aircraft, it being feared that if these were used for sorties into the North there would be a marked escalation of the conflict. After Tet, there was a scramble to build up the SVNAF, particularly its transport and helicopter capability, and further F-5s and A-37s were supplied. The US stopped short of providing anything more potent, however, particularly the much sought-after F-4 Phantom.

Top right:
A South Vietnamese Air Force pilot scrambles to his bomb-laden F-5A-25, 65-10556 (2×M177 750lb on the outer pylons, 2×Mk 82 500lb on the inners).

Centre right:
With the distinctive black and yellow checker rear fuselage band, F-5A-25 65-10558 gets airborne for another ground support mission. *Dorr*

Bottom right:
One of the SVNAF's F-5Bs, 65-10586. *via Dorr*

7 Canada's Own

On 6 February 1968 the first F-5 completed by Canadair Ltd was rolled out at the company's Cartierville plant near Montreal. Several hundred employees, government officials and military personnel witnessed the event, the assembled VIPs including the Hon Leo Cadieux, Canada's Minister of National Defence, and Gen J. V. Allard, Chief of the Defence Staff. A snowstorm could not blunt the significance of the event for Canada, whose armed forces had been integrated one week earlier. Although there were well-founded doubts over the wisdom of this move, at least the air force element could look forward to modernising its inventory, the F-5 representing the first of a new generation of combat aircraft.

Some time before the Canadian deal was finalised, Northrop added another national flag to the nose of its much-travelled F-5B demonstrator (63-8445), and late in 1967, numerous photographs of this aircraft appeared in the world's aeronautical press with 'RCAF' markings. Photos of at least four F-5As were also retouched to give the impression of service aircraft although the Royal Canadian Air Force had lost its autonomy by the time the CF-5 entered inventory.

Canadair was named prime contractor for the new Canadian Armed Forces fighter programme in July 1965, the CF-5 being given the company designation CL-219. The aircraft was to be powered by Orenda-built GE J85-15 engines which were of higher thrust — 4,300lb with afterburning — than their US counterparts. Orenda was then building the J85 under license for the CT-114 Tutor and production was expanded for the CF-5, the fighter engines taking the designation J85--CAN-15.

With major changes in the structure of the armed forces on the horizon, the CF-5 had not been the first choice as a partial replacement for the CF-104 by the RCAF. There was a marked preference for the more potent F-4 Phantom which was, however, considerably more expensive than the Northrop fighter; as the integration of the services was primarily a cost-saving exercise, the CF-5 was politically a better choice. It was a programme begun in a general atmosphere of compromise and was to continue to be subject to the changing political and economic climate.

Below left:
Northrop's demonstrator F-5B over dramatic natural scenery — believed to be on the Kootenay River, British Columbia — during its tour in the early 1960s. The Canadian 'markings of convenience' are of interest. *via Dorr*

Bottom left:
As well as the F-5B, Northrop decorated a number of F-5As in Canadian colours — and also retouched photos of early production aircraft, including the YF-5A — to publicise Canadian licence production. This is 63-8416, an F-5A-15. *via Dorr*

Above:
The F-5B demonstrator formates with a CL-41 Tutor during sales flights for the RCAF. In the event, CF-5s entered service after the integration of the Canadian services, and the RCAF designator was never carried by service aircraft. *Canadair via Hooks*

Below:
Roll-out for the first CF-5A at Cartierville. Stormy conditions were to reflect the controversy surrounding Canadian procurement and service use during the type's early career. *Robertson*

Canadair's agreement with Northrop as a license manufacturer covered 115 aircraft at a total cost of $215 million. About 80% of the programme was to be of Canadian origin and no allowance for cost escalation or resale rights was apparently made. In the same timescale it was widely announced that Canadair had also received an order from the Netherlands to build 105 aircraft for the Dutch air force — although some four years later, this deal was cited in a legal action brought by Northrop against the Canadian government, primarily over the sale of CF-5s to Venezuela. But in 1969, the Dutch order was a bonus to Canadair. It promised to cover any unforeseen cost escalation incurred during the production run of the Canadian aircraft, consisting of 89 CF-5A single-seaters and 26 CF-5D trainers.

Following the roll-out ceremony the camouflaged prototype CF-5A (116701) was shipped to the US to make its maiden flight from Edwards AFB in May 1968, piloted by Northrop's Hank Chouteau.

Edwards undertook extensive flight testing of the early production Canadian machines, which were significantly different to F-5As and F-5Bs built for MAP. Apart from the more powerful engines and some redesign of the air intakes to cope with the higher power, they had de-icing equipment, improved navigational and communications aids, together with an 87% increase in electrical generating capacity, and a lead-computing Ferranti type gyro-optical gunsight. A strengthened windscreen was fitted and the wing stores pylons made jettisonable; a runway arrester system was installed as standard, as was the necessary wiring and plumbing for an in-flight refuelling system. A two-position nosewheel leg increased the angle of attack by 3° and thereby reduced take-off run by 10-20%.

Above:
The first production CF-5D streams its drag 'chute after its first flight at Cartierville. *Canadair via Hooks*

The CF-5 could also accommodate a reconnaissance nose section with four cameras, as production of the first Canadair aircraft coincided with the maiden flight of the RF-5A, in May 1968. During the course of the Edwards tests the second production CF-5A (116702) was fitted with a 40in reconnaissance nose.

The result of a USAF/DoD development directive to Northrop in October 1963 calling for the reconnaissance capability that had been envisaged by the company for the N-156F, the new nose section was developed jointly by Northrop and W. Vinten Ltd of the UK. Each of the four KS-92A cameras had a 100ft film magazine and provided forward oblique, trimetrogen and split vertical coverage including horizon-to-horizon with overlap, through four viewfinder windows. The cameras and their film magazines were positioned far enough forward for the twin cannon to be retained and were reloaded via a forward hinged clamshell cover in the upper section of the nose. Associated equipment also located in the nose included four light sensors, defogging and cooling systems and a computer 'J' box. Early aircraft were also fitted with a pitot static nose boom.

Along with Canada, Norway acquired examples of the first production RF-5As, 16 of the initial 32 being supplied under MAP. Northrop also supplied Libya and Morocco without delay and eventually built 89 examples between June 1968 and June 1972.

In August 1968 the third CF-5 built became the first to fly from Montreal, this being CAF 116801, the first CF-5D. The year also saw the election of the liberal government of Pierre Trudeau. There followed a series of cutbacks in armed forces funding and manpower which were to have a significant effect on the CF-5 programme. The result was that only 54 were initially scheduled for operational service; although the full order for 118 aircraft was completed by Canadair nearly half the airframes were earmarked for storage and service on a rotational basis. This drastic move reduced the intended number of squadrons scheduled to fly the CF-5 from six to two. The action by the Canadian government regarding one of its foremost combat aircraft was regarded with amazement by outsiders, one foreign press report calling it 'a bizarre testimony to the vagaries of defence procurement'.

It became increasingly apparent that the integration plan for which Canada had such high hopes was not the model for the rest of the world to follow. There was a great deal of soul-searching among the air force element which saw its important part in the nation's defence suddenly lumped together with unfamiliar tasks previously the responsibility of other services that brought a whole new method of operating. But to its credit the CAF stuck with a dubious plan and saw it through, maintaining the high degree of professionalism for which Canadian military formations, particularly the air element, are known throughout the world.

The first CAF unit to re-equip with the CF-5 was No 434 'Bluenose' Squadron, which was re-activated on 15 February 1968 at CFB Cold Lake, Alberta. Having most recently flown the CF-104, No 434 had been stood down for more than a year. Its 'new look' extended to more than aircraft; with integration the familiar RAF style ranks and insignia gave way to Army ranks and a different chain of command to that of the RCAF. With the CF-5, the 'Bluenosers' would fly close air support, interdiction, photo reconnaissance and air superiority missions and at the same time be the primary source of CF-5 conversion training.

In preparation for the CF-5, 10 Canadian pilots went to Williams AFB in the summer of 1968 to be checked out on the F-5 under the auspices of the

Above:
**This rocket-launching aircraft is CF-5A (CF-116A)
116702, the second production example built by
Canadair.** *Wheeler*

4441st CCTS. Each man flew 30 hours' gunnery,
air combat, ground attack and night missions to
thoroughly familiarise himself with the new type.
Later that year CAF ground technicians and more
aircrews arrived in Arizona, in anticipation of the
first CF-5 deliveries back home.

No 434 Squadron received its first aircraft in
January 1969 and acceptances ran at three per
month thereafter, there being enough CF-5Bs on
hand by April to start the first conversion course in
Canada. In May the first conversion course was
held for the second squadron, No 433 'Porcupine'
at Bagotville, Quebec. This latter was a tactical
fighter squadron composed primarily of French-
speaking personnel and, unlike No 434, did not
have a dual training role.

The task of storing the CF-5s surplus to
immediate requirements fell mainly to the
Aerospace Maintenance Development Unit,
which was formed at CFB Trenton in 1967. It
provided a 'Maintenance organisation to predict
and plan methods of surmounting problems
associated with maintaining technical equipment
throughout the life-cycle of a weapons system'.
Also maintaining a sub-station at Mountainview,
southeast of Trenton, AMDU looked after the
CF-5 and other types, carrying out regular
inspections on individual airframes to determine
the average state of all aircraft of that type
remaining in CAF inventory.

By electing to rotate CF-5s in CAF service the
work necessary to 'pickle' airframes for long terms
— more than six months — storage has largely
been avoided by AMDU.

While working-up on the new type, No 434
Squadron recorded its first CF-5 loss when the
fourth production D model (116804) had to be
abandoned after both engines failed to re-light

during a training flight in March. The resultant
crash damaged the aircraft beyond repair. The
same month saw another roll-out ceremony at
Cartierville in the shape of the first NF-5A
(K-3001) for the Royal Netherlands Air Force, on
the 5th.

Going Dutch
The Koninklijke Nederlandse Luchtmacht's
associated with the F-5 began in 1966 when an
extensive evaluation was made of types that were
likely to replace its F-84s and T-33s. It was hoped
that the type chosen could be manufactured largely
in Holland by Fokker-VFW but in the event this
proved too costly an option. With the F-5 selected
as the winner of the evaluation, the KLu signed a
co-operative manufacturing agreement between
Canadair, Fokker and Avio Diepen at Ypenburg.
Under this, Avio and Fokker produced fuselage
sections and tail assemblies and shipped them to
Canadair for final assembly. A letter of intent to
purchase 75 NF-5A single-seaters and 30 two-seat
NF-5Bs was signed on 30 January 1967.

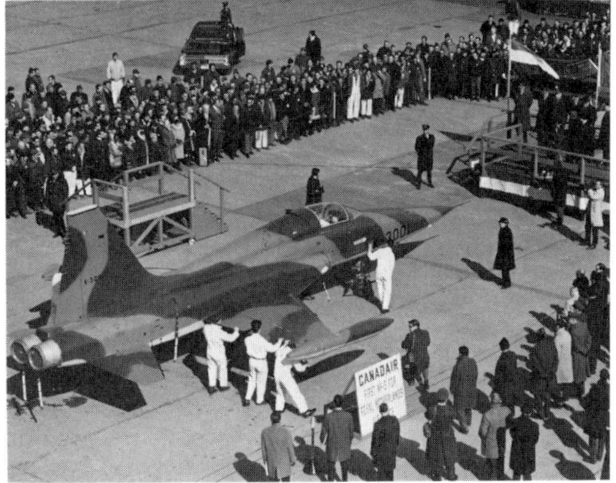

Above:
**As the billboard says, K-3001 was the first NF-5A for the
Netherlands.** *Canadair via Hooks*

There were hopes that Belgium would also select the F-5 for its future requirements, thereby leading to a degree of standardisation in NATO-assigned air forces, with benefits to industry through licence manufacturing agreements. Belgium instead chose the Mirage 5, and it was not to be until the advent of the F-16 that standardisation in Europe improved.

Having selected the NF-5, the Dutch air force sent selected personnel to Canada for conversion training under the guidance of the CAF. Four Dutch pilots were among a class of 25 going through the No 434 Squadron 'school' in the summer and autumn of 1969, and five more Dutch officers followed later in the year, the intention being for a nucleus of trained personnel to initiate NF-5 conversion courses in Holland as soon as practicable. No 331 Squadron RNethAF was formed for this purpose in 1970.

Technically the Dutch F-5s were the most advanced of the series to date: an important new feature was the leading edge manoeuvring flaps incorporated in a stronger wing structure. When set for high-speed manoeuvring, the electrically operated leading and trailing edge flaps are synchronised by a control box which sets flap travel limits and has indicator inputs. The flaps, normally operated manually by a lever, are then controlled by a two-position thumb-operated switch on the starboard throttle lever. When the manual control lever is set in the fully down position, the switch is bypassed and a protective switch in the circuit also prevents the flaps from being lowered to the manoeuvring settings at speeds above 460kt IAS.

The two-position nosewheel oleo and airfield arrester system were fitted as standard and the strengthened wing enabled more ordnance to be carried on ejector sub-racks fitted to wing and fuselage pylons. Up to 229Imp gal of fuel can be carried in external tanks. Electrically-actuated doors helped increase mass airflow on take-off and six louvred 'air doors' were positioned in each fuselage side aft of the wing trailing edge to provide additional air cooling.

NF-5 pilots also had the benefit of Doppler radar navigation, an attitude heading and reference

system, emergency UHF radio, and a radio altimeter. The Doppler uses an on-board computer to provide digital on-track and across-track distance information based on radar inputs.

The Dutch order aircraft were identified by Canadair as the CL-226, the first A model making its maiden flight on 24 March 1969, with company test pilot W. Longhurst at the controls. The first NF-5B flew on 7 July, in the hands of S. Grossman, and the RNethAF officially took delivery of the first machine in October.

It was decided to fly each NF-5 to Holland; the first four set off from Bagotville on 7 November, following a polar route. The quartet of two-seaters flew to Goose Bay, Labrador, thence to Sondestrom in Greenland, Keflavik in Iceland and Lossiemouth in Scotland before the final leg to Twenthe AB. En route the Dutch fighter bomber/trainers were watched over by the USAF's 2nd Aircraft Delivery Group, which provided operational briefings and stationed a C-130 SAR aircraft along the track followed by the NF-5s. The delivery flights went under the general name 'High Flight' and consisted of sections of four to six aircraft. The Hercules, nick-named 'Duck Butt', provided bearings at predetermined points and carried para-medical teams in the event of a 'worst case' mishap over water or rugged, remote territory.

The delivery flights continued until March 1972. All NF-5s arrived safely, only one flight recording an incident. This occurred on the 16th such operation, in the autumn of 1971. Some 30 minutes after leaving Keflavik and approaching the rendezvous point with the C-130, Capt C. J. van Holstein reported difficulty in maintaining formation and some loss of vision. The flight was then at the point of no return — with some 300 miles of open water to cross before reaching Scotland.

Capt van Holstein tried breathing 100% oxygen, but there was no improvement in his condition. With the paramed team on board the Hercules standing by and being kept informed by van

K-3011
K-3038
K-3042
K-3008

RESCUE

Holstein's No 2, Lt Sneek, the flight proceeded. But van Holstein's problems grew worse. Lt Sneek noticed his leader's speech becoming impaired and that his hearing had apparently deteriorated as well. To conserve fuel Lt Sneek elected to remain at 33,000ft and keep station with van Holstein's aircraft.

Approaching the Scottish coast, the Dutch pilot's problems were compounded further by being unable to contact Moray radar. He requested his formation leader, flying some 10 minutes ahead, to relay an emergency call. At 180 miles out Lt Sneek made contact with Moray radar and the two NF-5s started a slow descent to 20,000ft in close formation. Capt van Holstein was still in a bad way, with his field of vision being confined to the centre of his instrument panel. Luckily the weather at Lossiemouth was good and the Dutchmen were given a straight in approach. His eyesight having improved a little, van Holstein was able to respond to talk-down instructions passed by Lt Sneek, but only lined up with the runway after considerable effort. At 180kt IAS at 1,500ft the gear and flaps went down. All was well until van Holstein's aircraft passed the approach lights. It suddenly sank. 'Pull up! Pull up!' yelled Sneek.

Hardly conscious by this time, van Holstein complied. Seconds later he was over the runway centre-line and instinctively put on more power. The aircraft settled and rolled — but Lt Sneek had to shout three times for his leader to activate the braking parachute. After turning off the runway Capt van Holstein had to be hoisted out of his aircraft; subsequent medical tests showed that he had suffered an acute malfunction of the inner ear which upset his balance. Fortunately he made a complete recovery.

In the meantime, the CAF Freedom Fighter training programme was proceeding, No 434 Squadron gradually expanding its expertise in the many roles planned for the CF-5. A primary consideration was to use the aircraft for reinforcement of forces defending the Northern Flank of Europe and in 1970 the squadron flew the first of many overseas deployments, Operation 'Fence Phase 1', destination Scotland.

The first appearance of the CF-5 at a tactical air meet took place in October 1970 and from the 19th to the 23rd, No 434 Squadron carried off all the trophies, including that for the top tactical squadron. Two cross-Canada speed records were established in the summer of 1970 when Capts Jake Miller and Ron Small flew their CF-5s from Victoria to Sheerwater, a distance of 2,800 miles. At an average speed of 636mph Miller completed the flight in four hours 24 minutes 53 seconds. Then on 1 July 1970 Capt Pat Pattison set an east-to-west record from Sheerwater to Victoria in five hours 34 minutes 21 seconds. This flight was to commemorate the 50th anniversary of the first cross-Canada mail flight in 1920, when it took 10½ days.

Behind the scenes, work was underway to give the CF-5 the capability to reach NATO air bases in Europe without time-consuming refuelling stops. Northrop supplied the probes for the CF-5s and these were fitted by CAF technicians at Cold Lake, but it was some time before a tanker was available for their use. No tankers were purchased and instead the CAF modified two of its CC-137 transports to a tanker configuration tailored to its own requirements. Aircraft from No 437 Squadron Air Transport Command had centre wing tanks installed with a capacity of 60,000lb of fuel and pumps and piping to feed it to Beech Aircraft Corp 1080 pods slung beneath each wingtip. Each pod had a metal boom attachment from which 35ft of flexible hose was trailed, the CF-5 pilot flying his probe into the metal basket on the end of each hose. Unlike USAF/SVNAF F-5Cs, the CF-5's probe was fitted on the starboard side of the nose.

Despite needing some 18 months to perfect — including design and manufacture of hoses and baskets and time to rectify early faults — the CAF's aerial refuelling system gave the CF-5 sufficient range to reach Europe without needing to land, each of the CC-137s being able to replenish two CF-5s simultaneously. Maximum fuel transfer rate was 2,000lb per minute and on a typical overseas sortie each CF-5 took on up to 6,000lb of fuel. Pilots needed an average of three hours to perfect the fuel transfer technique, making several wet and dry contacts in that time.

The CC-137s thus became an integral part of CAF CF-5 long range operations, giving a considerable boost to the policy of 'quick reaction'. In addition to their tanker role the modified Boeing 707s acted as 'mother ships', briefing fighter pilots on weather conditions along their intended route, handling communications and keeping an eye on the fuel burn rate of their charges.

Top left:
The fourth production NF-5A formates with aircraft No 12 and two others from well into the production run. *Wheeler*

Inset:
A close-up of the starboard side refuelling probe of a CF-5A during cold weather trials. *Canadian Aviation*

Left:
A pair of CF-5As hook up to one of the CAF's Boeing CC-137s (13704) with its unique Beech fuel transfer system in operation. *Canadian Aviation*

In November 1972 No 434 Squadron checked out half its squadron pilots in air-to-air refuelling, the CC-137 flying up from its base at Trenton. It returned in December to help qualify the remainder and the unit prepared for its first overseas deployment to put their training into practice. This came on 6 June the following year as Exercise 'Long Leap I'. Five aircraft positioned at Bagotville for the sortie to be joined by the two tankers. The No 434 Squadron machines were then joined by four CF-5s from No 433 and the deployment got underway on the 9th, their destination Andoya in Norway. The trip proved uneventful and the Canadian crews gained valuable experience of European operational procedures by flying up to 20 sorties per day until 19 June when they began their return flight.

No 434's training mission had meanwhile been extended to pilots and technicians from Venezuela, that country having agreed to purchase 20 CF-5s (16 CF-5As and four CF-5Ds) on 7 October 1971. The contract, worth $35 million including support equipment and spares, was finalised on 14 December 1971 and arrangements were made to accommodate Venezuelan pilots and ground crews at Cold Lake. Their training started on 10 January 1972 while AMDU prepared their aircraft, and on the same day a Venezuelan AF C-130, which had brought the men to Canada, returned home with spares and equipment.

The first four aircraft (two CF-5As and two CF-5Ds) were officially handed over at Trenton and they left for Venezuela on 11 February, piloted by Canadians as no nationals had had time to receive sufficient training to undertake such a long trip. The aircraft, routed via South Carolina, Florida and Puerto Rico, had reached their destination on 14 February. Logistic support was provided by a Venezuelan C-130 which also ferried a team of Canadians led by Maj Doug Pickering, which was to remain in South America for six months to establish an 'in-country' training programme and operate a CF-5 operational training unit.

There were three delivery flights, under the codename Operation 'Canamigo'; the second left on 12 April — eight aircraft arriving two days later — and the last took place on 7 June when six

aircraft departed Trenton. The CF-5 which, along with nine Mirages also purchased in 1972, represented a significant boost to Venezuela's air force inventory, both aircraft then being the most modern acquired. The CF-5s (one of which was later given reconnaissance capability and became an RCF-5A) were initially based at El Libertador on Lake Valencia. They subsequently moved to Vicente Landaeta and currently equip Escuadron de Caza Nos 34 and 35. Two CF-5Ds arrived in the country in late 1973 and the other in 1974. These were not additional aircraft but the last of the original order.

Although this deal with Venezuela was welcomed by Canadair, which at the time had sufficient CF-5s to meet future CAF needs and could easily afford to release 20, especially if they earned revenue, Northrop subsequently refuted any right to sell. In 1974 the US company sued the Canadian government for $17.5 million, primarily over resale rights, and royalties on the entire programme because costs increased during the CF-5 production run. In 1972 the government agreed to pay Canadair a cost over-run and tried to recover this from Northrop, which refused. While some agreement was reached between Canadair and the government, the latter filed a countersuit against Northrop for $26 million. Other factors pertaining to the CF-5 programme were cited and at the time it appeared that litigation would drag on for some years. However, the matter was finally settled out of court when the Canadian government paid Northrop $9 million.

Canada's commitment to NATO was emphasised in the 1971 Defence White Paper, which provided for the CF-5 to deploy to Europe for an 'exploratory operation' to determine the suitability of the aircraft for this duty. Accordingly in mid-October 1970 six aircraft had flown to Baden Soellingen and carried out operational trials in their primary role of ground support and the secondary ones of reconnaissance and interception.

Flown by pilots from both CAF squadrons the CF-5s arrived at Prestwick on 16 November and were stored by Scottish Aviation in preparation for a second series of trials in Norway. (SAL maintains a major overhaul, repair and storage depot for CAF aircraft in Europe.) Two left for Rygge on 27 January 1971, followed by the remaining four on the 28th. All six returned to Prestwick on 23 February and were stored until their return to Canada in June.

The result of these trials was a willingness to commit the CF-5s to Allied Command Europe in an emergency, one squadron being available to Allied Mobile Force (Air), the other to support a Canadian air and sea transportable combat group earmarked for operations in Denmark and Norway. Both Nos 433 and 434 Squadrons were augmented by further aircraft for this commitment, and photographic reconnaissance training was revised to include coastal surveillance flights over Canadian territorial waters.

Facing page, top left:
NATO co-operation. CF-5A 16750 takes on fuel from a RAF No 90 Squadron Victor tanker. *MoD via Wheeler*

Facing page, top right:
CAF CF-5A pilots watch the refuelling technique of a Lightning T4, again using Victor K2 XH588.
MoD via Wheeler

Facing page, bottom:
CF-5As lined up at Plattsburg AFB, New York on 26 June 1976. The nearest machine was then part of No 433 Squadron. *Dorr*

Below:
The moose badge of No 419 Squadron adorns this CF-5D (CF-116D) in aggressor camouflage, complete with WarPac-style nose numbers that are a feature of most Canadian and US aggressor F-5s. *Canadian Aviation*

8 Tiger II

By the late 1960s, Northrop had enough data on F-5A/B performance to propose a second generation version incorporating significant technical advances in a similar size airframe. Principally the changes would centre on providing the F-5 with improved interception capability based on radar, more wing area to improve manoeuvrability, and more powerful engines.

General Electric had developed the J85 to give 5,000lb of thrust under a growth programme for the engine that had begun as far back as 1962 with experimental tests. An entirely new, larger compressor was on test by 1963 and during 1964 the sixth production F-5B was leased to GE for engine test bed work. GE's Virgil Weaver, who headed a flight test group at Edwards, implemented work on new engine bays for the aircraft and the team also fabricated enlarged air intakes and extended the wings by inserting root sections, in conjunction with Northrop engineers and aerodynamists. With the J85-GE-21 engines installed, 68-8445 became the YF-5B-21. John Fritz, then GE's chief of flight test, was scheduled to undertake the first flight, on 28 March 1969.

Came the dawn of first flight day — and the aircraft was not ready. Later that morning it was still up on jacks but as the team were committed to fly the aircraft that day, they continued to work feverishly. By 3pm all was ready and Fritz climbed the ladder and strapped himself into the front seat for the first taxi runs. Minor problems showed up and took nearly two hours to fix. Consequently it was evening before the aircraft took off for the first time. But all the work culminated in success; Fritz climbed down after his 40-minute flight and gave the traditional 'thumbs up'.

There followed 130 hours further testing, not only of the engines but other design features that would be incorporated in the new F-5. These included the two-position nosewheel oleo devel-

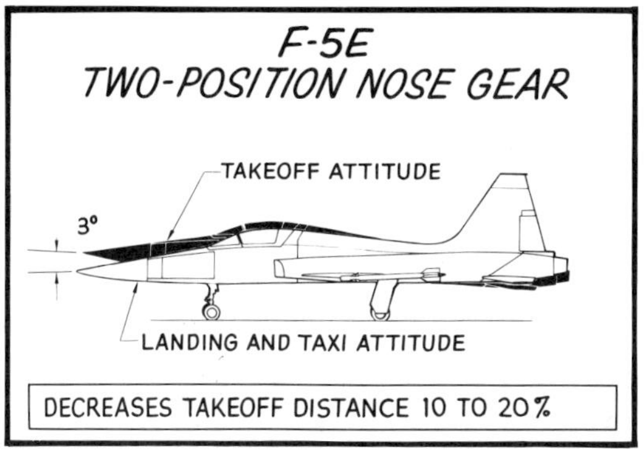

Below left:
Northrop shipped 64-13317 back from Vietnam and dis-assembled it to determine how well the F-5A stood up to the rigours of combat. It passed into the inventory of the 425th TFTS, 58th FTW and was seen at Forbes AFB in October 1971, as the mount of Lt-Col Bob Whitener. The aircraft was subsequently flown to McClellen AFB for onward shipment to Taiwan. *George Pennick*

Bottom left:
The first F-5E, appropriately marked with a tiger's head. Subtle contour refinement is much in evidence, although from some angles both F-5 single-seaters looked very similar. Only flying it would demonstrate the major improvements made. *via Dorr*

Below:
Ground crew marshalling one of the 425th TFTS's F-5Es at Williams AFB. *via Hooks*

oped for the CF-5 and plenum chamber (auxiliary air) doors positioned in the fuselage sides aft of the wings. These early tests were to stand Northrop in good stead in the next stage of the new fighter's development.

Northrop's approach to the Department of Defense outlining the proposed F-5 update was accepted with the proviso that the company furnish full flight test reports showing that the aircraft would still retain the primary selling points of the existing model, especially its ease of handling, reliability and cost-effective maintainability. It was felt that to depart radically from this proven concept would be detrimental to MAP and FMS programmes, many customer countries for the developed fighter being assumed to be those currently operating the F-5A.

Before making any official decision, the DoD called for a competition for an 'Advanced International Fighter', thus obliging the Air Force to solicit proposals from industry before allocating any FY 1970 funds for development. The competition was made known to industry on 26 February 1970 and by March three companies besides Northrop had responded: McDonnell Douglas put forward a stripped version of the F-4E Phantom, Lockheed the CL-1200 Lancer based on the F-104, and LTV proposed a lightweight development of the F-8 Crusader known as the V-100. All these latter were 'paper' projects.

The international fighter evaluation took six

months, at the end of which time the Secretary of Defense approved production of the Northrop design as the F-5E, the new suffix being allocated in January 1971, a few weeks after the initial contract was issued on 8 December 1970. This covered five pre-service development aircraft and 325 production models on a definitive fixed-price incentive basis. While the USAF correctly estimated that Northrop's costings for the F-5E were too low, the programme did not turn out to be as expensive as the Air Force predicted and as production got underway the price of the F-5E was to settle down to approximately $2.1 million per copy.

Northrop experienced some delay in completing the first pre-production evaluation aircraft when titanium forgings were found to be necessary for the aft fuselage engine exhaust shroud, and to accelerate the programme during the flight testing phase the Air Force asked for six aircraft rather than five, in November 1971.

Although the USAF had shown great confidence in the J85-21 meeting its quoted performance figure — indeed it was recommended as the powerplant for late-production F-5As under a contract change notice issued to Northrop as early as January 1969 — some time would elapse before the engine was finally cleared for installation in the F-5E. But on 11 August 1972 the maiden flight of the first F-5E (71-1417) took place at Edwards. Hank Chouteau took the aircraft up for 50 minutes, reaching over 20,000ft in the process. Afterwards he said, 'The minute you release the brakes you get the feeling the airplane thinks its airborne'.

The USAF began evaluation tests at Edwards on 18 August; they began well enough but had to be suspended between 21 September and 16 December while engine modifications were carried out. These required new static testing before flight which were not completed until 25 April 1973 when the first F-5E was accepted by the Air Force.

Full scale airframe fatigue tests continued at Hawthorne and had reached 10,000 hours or 2½ service lifetimes by the autumn of 1974. Northrop

extended fatigue tests through four lifetimes and USAF evaluation of the six test F-5Es had accumulated 1,350 hours in 1,750 flights by that autumn.

Once again the 425th TFTS was the first recipient of the new F-5 model, the unit gradually working up to a monthly utilisation rate of 28.5 hours per aircraft by the early summer of 1974.

Among the systems flight tested by the evaluation aircraft was the LATAR — Laser Augmented Target Acquisition & Recognition System. Located under the forward fuselage, it comprised a laser target designator, a spot tracker and an electro-optical sensor. The third machine (71-1419) conducted flights with LATAR and Maverick and Sidewinder missile armament.

The performance of the F-5E showed a significant improvement over the F-5A and by specifically tailoring it to meet an increased quality of fighter threat facing the Free World, Northrop designed it to give its best in the envelope where air combat has invariably taken place — from Mach 0.4 to 1.4 and from 35,000ft to ground level. For combat the aircraft retained a pair of M-39 revolver-type cannon with a total of 560 rounds of 20mm ammunition and wingtip-mounted AIM-9 Sidewinder AAMs.

An Emerson AN/APQ-153 (later AN/APQ-

GENERAL DESCRIPTION
F-5E Internal Arrangement

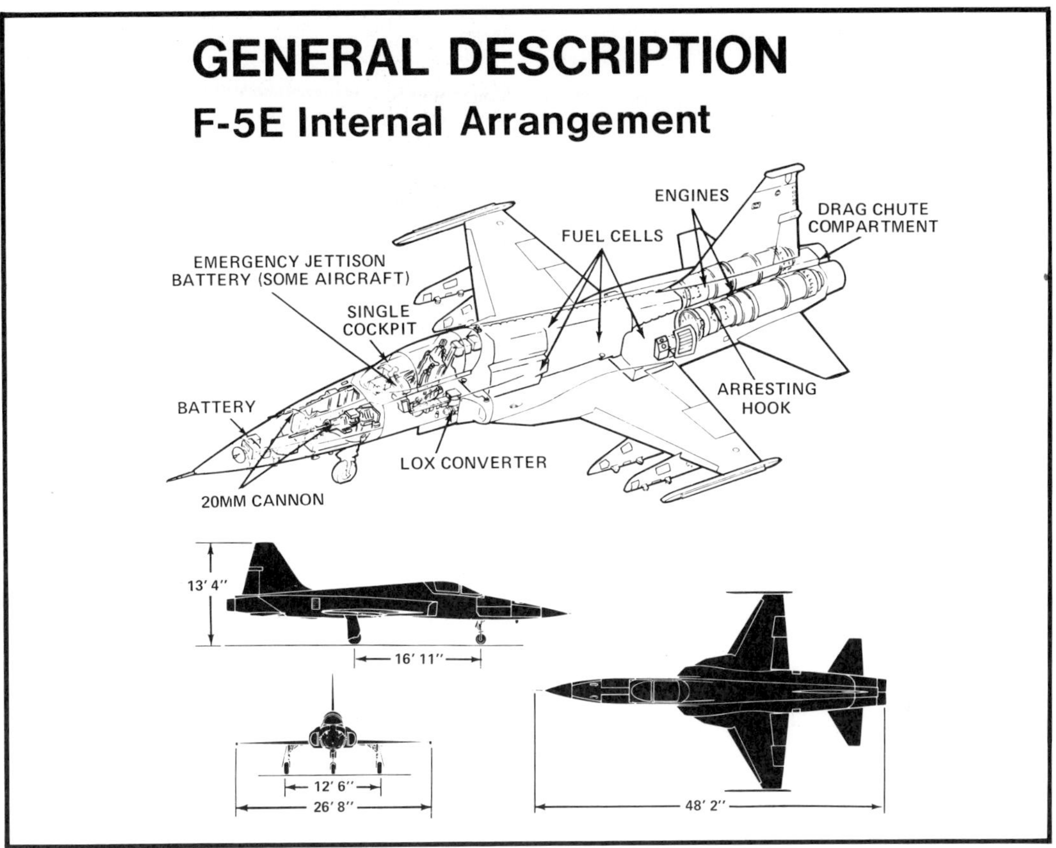

159[V]) radar and General Electric ASG-29 gyro gunsight (later ASG-31 lead computing sight) constituted the fire control system, the radar accomplishing search and range tracking even in ground clutter and provided range-rate inputs to the lead-computing optical sight systems (LCOSS). When the pilot depressed the radar acquisition button the radar achieved lock-on. The range analogue on the gunsight computed the variables of aerial gunfiring, down to the minimal range of 1,000ft, at which point a signal appeared in the diamond-shaped reticle.

When committed to a firing pass, the pilot raised the guard cover of the gun/camera switch and pushed the toggle to 'guns and camera', making the trigger live and arming the gun camera to automatically record the sight reticle relative to the target. To overcome any difficulty in keeping the pipper on target, there was a snap-shoot option, allowing the pilot to move the pipper towards the target and fire as the two were about to merge. In-range indication began at 2,700ft.

As the trigger was depressed, the gun gas doors just forward of each M-39 barrel opened to disperse gases. As pilots found in Vietnam with the F-5C, if hot gun gas is allowed to enter the air intakes, engine stalls and damage could occur. Even so, the F-5E's firing pass was spectacular. The second the firing trigger was depressed, it felt as though 'the whole front of the aircraft has turned into a pneumatic jackhammer' as one pilot put it. Gunsmoke rushed past the canopy and some of it invariably seeped into the cockpit as the M-39s pumped out shells at a rate of 1,500 rounds per minute.

Top left:
The heart of the F-5E was the J85-21 engine of 5,000lb thrust, one of which is seen here being slotted into the rear fuselage of an aircraft at Palmdale in 1974. Built at GE's Aircraft Engine Group at Lynn, Massachusetts, more than 10,000 J85s had been made for the T-38/F-5 series by that time.

Left:
The third production F-5E taking off to flight test the Laser Augmented Target Acquisition & Recognition (LATAR) system developed by Northrop. The pod of the system is positioned under the front fuselage and this particular test recorded the interface between LATAR and an electro-optical missile, in this case, Maverick.
via Door

To make maximum use of the 7.4:1 thrust-to-weight ratio, each J85-21 had a new nine-stage titanium corrosion-proof compressor. The engines, which were virtually smokeless, were fed by fixed geometry intakes with rear fuselage auxiliary inlets providing maximum thrust levels for take-off and low speed operation.

The fuselage was 15in longer than the F-5A and was also 16in wider to accommodate each extra compressor stage. The enlarged air intakes increased air flow from 44lb/sec to 52lb/sec, and the extra fuselage space enabled the fitting of larger fuel cells, resulting in a total tankage increase of 570lb (from 585 US gal to 671 US gal).

The F-5E's wing remained 'dry', the area being increased from 170sq ft to 186.2sq ft by means of a structural plug inserted between the two wing halves at the roots. Span was thus increased to 26ft 8in including AIM-9 launch rails. The leading edge extension was also enlarged to equal 4.4% of the basic wing area, resulting in a 38% boost in maximum lift. The wing also incorporated the leading edge manoeuvring flaps developed for the NF-5A; these provided for a maximum droop angle of 24° forward and 20° at the the trailing edge for landing and take-off or manoeuvring below speeds of 200kt IAS. Typical settings for air combat were 18° fore and 16° aft in the 200-250kt IAS speed range, or respectively 12° to 8° for use above 250kt IAS.

The avionics fit comprised UHF command radio; UHF automatic D/F; AN/AIC-18 intercommunications and AN/APX-72 IFF/SIF. AN/ARN-56 TACAN was supplemented by a SST-181 X-band radar transponder (Skyspot) and a solid-state attitude and heading reference system, although INS, LF/MF automatic D/F, VOR/ILS and VHF communications could be fitted according to customer specification.

Each F-5E for MAP/FMS customers came with a 'delivery package' which included five external stores pyons, two wingtip missile launchers, one 265gal external fuel tank and one loose items kit container. Optional equipment apart from avionics extended to 275gal and 150gal wing tanks, the 50gal wingtip tanks, an inflight refuelling system, and the photo reconnaissance nose. Pylon jettison conversion kits were classed as 'war readiness material' and along with weapons had to be ordered under agreements with the US government rather than Northrop.

In addition, the F-5E customer could, as with the early models, take advantage of the pilot and maintenance personnel training programme, either in the USA or the user country, depending on preference. For training maintenance personnel in the user country, Northrop could also supply a range of mobile training sets to duplicate aircraft systems. By the time the F-5E was available, Northrop's product support programme could provide skilled technical assistance through a network of agents worldwide.

Northrop took 70-1390, the 10th production Tiger II, to the 1973 Paris Salon, the aircraft being brilliantly demonstrated by Bob Hoover of North American Rockwell. Appropriately decorated with a tiger's head on a blue vertical tail band and show number 65, the aircraft confirmed its potential for the countries already interested in obtaining it in quantity.

Tiger Foxtrot

Shortly after the USAF formally accepted the first F-5E, Northrop instigated a full scale development programme for a two-seat version which, like its F-5B forbear, would retain the full combat capability of the single-seater. It had not originally been the company's intention to offer a two-seat version of the F-5E, but after initial flight tests of the fighter, the performance differential between it and the F-5B was significantly wide; foreign air force customers were of the same opinion, and so to meet what quickly became a definite requirement, Northrop married the F-5E's performance to a trainer version, the F-5F.

Once again the reconfiguration was confined mainly to the fuselage, which was stretched by 42in in the nose area to accommodate the second cockpit, raised 10in above the front one as in the F-5B and T-38. A full set of flight controls was provided in the rear position, including a radar display, although the lead computing optical sight system was deleted, only the front cockpit being provided with the LCOSS. As an alternative to a human occupant, the second seat position could be used for a laser designator and other advanced electronics equipment.

In one respect the F-5F differs noticeably from the F-5B in that it is the only two-seater of the series to be armed — albeit with one rather than two M-39 guns. With less available space in the nose bays the bulky cannon and its 140-round ammunition tank were restricted to the port side with a single access door, although the tubular

Top right:
The panel of the F-5E showing the considerable equipment instrumentation that had been added since the first T-38s flew.

Above right:
Up to 20 F-5Es were being produced at Hawthorne by the time of this photograph in January 1974.

Right:
A striking view of a F-5E going heaven-wards during a flight test from Palmdale in November 1974. *via Hooks*

F-5F Internal Arrangement

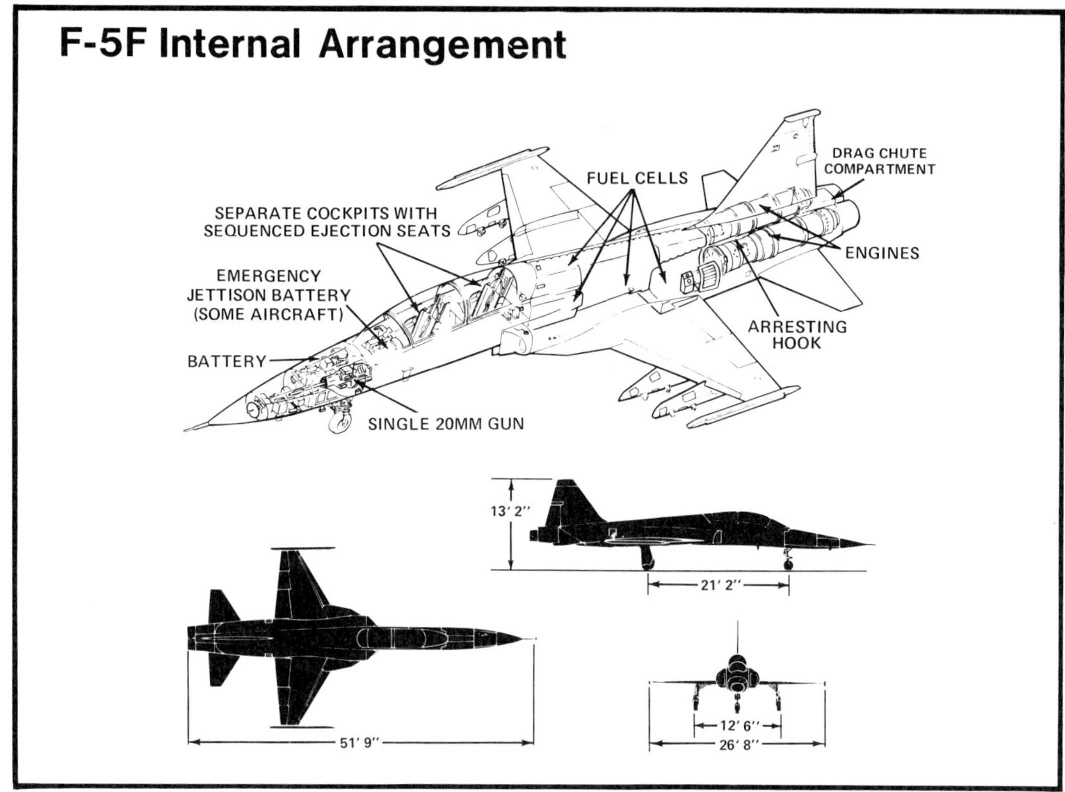

'barrel' of a ram-air equipment cooling intake was positioned in the starboard side cannon port.

Other changes made to the F-5F were the provision of ballast weights designed for bolting under the rear fuselage immediately forward of the jet exhaust to compensate for nose-heaviness of the radar and the second seat. Wing fences were positioned at approximately mid-span.

The first F-5F (73-889) made its maiden flight from Edwards on 25 September 1974 piloted by Nothrop test pilot Dick Thomas. No major problems were encountered on the 43-minute flight, the aircraft reaching 23,500ft and a speed of Mach 0.8, and the F-5F joined the F-5E/F Joint Test Force at Edwards for thorough pre-service evaluation which ended with spin tests in the autumn of 1975. The second F-5F (73-890) flew the same day.

TigerEye

To provide a reconnaissance capability for the F-5E, Northrop originally specified the RF-5A interchangeable nose. But with very few other aircraft able to carry cameras and sensors as integral installations — the trend was very much towards podded surveillance systems — Northrop began studies into a 'dedicated' F-5E reconnaissance model in the mid-1970s. The company funded development as a private venture, estimating the potential market for such a variant to be worth between $750 million and $1 billion.

The test vehicle was production F-5E 71-1420 which retained armament and housed cameras and sensors in an elongated 10ft nose section which provided 26cu ft of space — nearly nine times more than that of the RF-5A. In order to avoid drag-inducing fairings, the cameras were grouped in a slim nose section which retained the shark-like contours of the original. To overcome the lack of space the cameras were grouped on pallets installed through a V-shaped door on the underside. The basic fit was three pallets for low-to-medium altitude day/night photography, low or high level panoramic, and medium range stand-off/long range oblique photography.

A KS-87B frame camera could be positioned in the extreme nose, which had an optically-flat viewing window for oblique forward, line of flight work. Access to the nose was achieved by means of sliding the cone forward on rails. The 5ft long main bay had V-shaped lower windows providing 190° horizon-to-horizon coverage, the cameras being loaded and removed through the hinge-down dorsal door and four side hatches.

Northrop aimed to fly the reconnaissance-configured prototype in less than a year after US

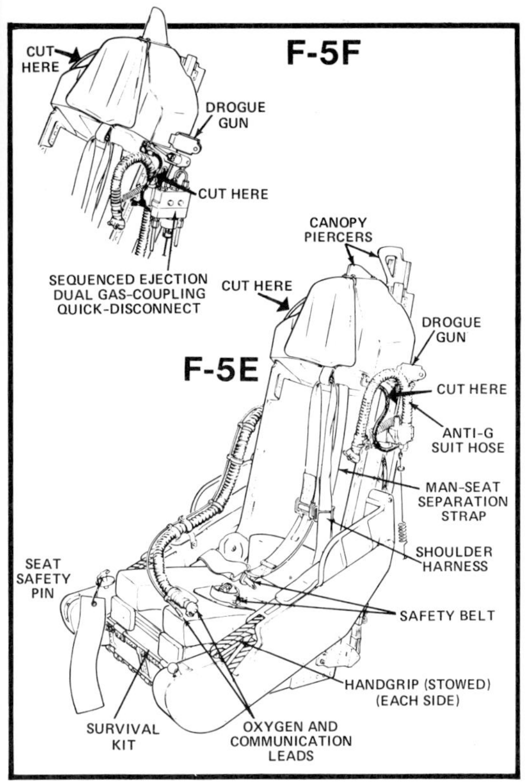

Below:
You can almost hear the band playing as the test pilot crew march to the first production F-5F, neatly positioned on its star base. At this stage, the aircraft lacked wing fences.

Below right:
Northrop technicians prepare the prototype RF-5E (71-1420) for its first flight. Note the excellent access to the pallet-mounted nose cameras. No armament is in evidence here, although production RF-5Es do retain the twin cannon. *via Hooks*

government approval for the work was confirmed in March 1978. That target was achieved ahead of time, 71-1420 taking to the air for the first time on 29 January 1979. Flight evaluation was conducted from Northrop's flight test facility at Edwards, with the USAF's Fighter/Attack Systems Programme Office at Wright-Patterson monitoring progress.

The 425th Tactical Fighter Training Squadron at Williams was again the first unit to test this new F-5 production model, the first arriving on 4 April 1975. The aim was to have a full squadron operational before the end of the year to initiate the training of foreign pilots. A year later, Welko Gasich, then Vice President of Northrop's aircraft group, stated that although customers were quite happy with the mid-1970s capability of the Tiger II there would undoubtedly come a time when increased capability in the form of avionics packages and sophisticated weapons would be required. The majority of these were to manifest themselves in the ultimate development of the F-5E, initially known as the F-5G and powered by a single F404 engine. The designation was subsequently changed not only to reflect the considerable difference between the two models, but to conform with modern designation numbers for the US fighters. Thus was born the F-20 Tigershark.

To enhance the F-5E's capabilities through the remainder of the 1980s and the 1990s, numerous systems have been tested in line with standard development programmes. Among these is the tailoring of the MBB sub-munitions dispenser pod designed for the Panavia Tornado, to the F-5E's centreline pylon. All that is required, says the German company, is pylon wiring and a cockpit control unit; the Modular Dispenser System (MDS) was tested over the Eglin AFB ranges in a Tiger II and other aircraft in September and October 1985.

9 New Tigers for Old

The advent of the F-5E gave a number of nations their first modern jet combat aircraft, while others updated their inventories of F-5A/B models more or less on a basis of one-for-one replacement. In most cases however, previous users opted to increase their orders for the more capable Tiger II — indeed for Korea and Nationalist China the aircraft became the cornerstone of their air defence.

The End in Vietnam
Although the SVNAF continued to expand after the Tet offensive of 1968 and the sortie rate went up dramatically compared to three years before, there was still great reliance on the massive firepower of US air forces. American withdrawals began in 1969, by which time an Improvement & Modernisation Plan for the SVNAF was becoming quite evident, both in terms of aircraft and personnel.

By 1970 the Vietnamese were taking over more and more responsibility for the air war, backed by an all-out training programme: the Air Force flew 40% of all sorties over South Vietnam that year. Build-up of the F-5 force was slow at first and by 1973 there were still only 35 in inventory. Prestigious as the F-5s were, the South Vietnamese understandably concentrated greater effort in boosting their helicopter and fixed wing troop transport capability to continue the 'in country' anti-guerilla war along US lines.

By establishing its own training command and greatly expanding maintenance facilities the SVNAF developed a support organisation and to some extent centralised operational planning of combat operations. Since 1969, ground attack sorties had been vested in the second jet type, the A-37, over 200 of which were available. Useful though the Dragonfly was, the last thing the Vietnamese really needed at that stage of the war was yet another type to burden the support facilities. Under Vietnamisation the overall inventory represented 25 different types of aircraft — challenge enough for a large well-organised air force, let alone one short on experience and trying at the same time to fight a war.

Increasing US troop withdrawals in the early 1970s led the North Vietnamese to attempt a conventional invasion of the South in March 1972. Largely broken by US airpower with able support from the SVNAF, this incursion bred a dangerous and false sense of security in the South Vietnamese — despite events on the political front they remained convinced that the US would always be on hand to back them. A ceasefire came into effect in early 1973, prior to which the Americans poured aircraft and other equipment into the country so that Vietnam would — theoretically at least — be able to stand on its own if the fighting flared up again.

Part of this flood included more F-5As, a total of 126 from Korea, Iran and Taiwan arriving to boost

strength to an eventual eight squadrons in the 23rd Wing. In the ensuing 18 months the North bided its time, moving men and material south, equipment inventories swelling with Russian-supplied SA-2 and SA-7 ground-to-air missiles, and 37mm and 57mm anti-aircraft artillery.

With the American political turmoil surrounding Watergate diverting attention from Vietnam, the SVNAF continued sporadic action as the ceasefire was repeatedly broken; by 1972 there were 60 squadrons on hand, the bulk of its aircraft supplied under Operations 'Enhance' and 'Enhance Plus'. The latter brought South Vietnam its first F-5Es, 18 aircraft having been diverted from orders scheduled for Iran and in conspicous desert camouflage. Reports suggest however that the SVNAF had little chance to use the increased capability offered by the F-5E and subsequent action was almost exclusively undertaken by the earlier model, due mainly to the fact that the F-5E required considerably more skilled ground support, particularly for its radar-based fire control system.

Bottom left:
USAF Staff Sgt Donald L. Niles photographed this SVNAF F-5B in its hardened shelter at Bien Hoa in April 1971. *USAF*

Top:
Hectic activity at Tan Son Nhut air base on 6 November 1973 as Operation 'Enhance Plus' delivers more F-5s to the air force that then had some 18 months of existence left. On the K-loader is F-5A-15 63-8383, ex-Iranian AF. *Sgt R. Sullivan, USAF*

Above left:
After unloading, the later SVNAF aircraft were placed in barbed-wire compounds pending final assembly. This group was at Bien Hoa during 'Enhance Plus' and includes 63-8385 (F-5A-15); 65-10482 (F-5A-25); and 65-10536 (F-5A-25), all of which were previously operated by the IIAF. *USAF*

Above right:
An eight-pack element ready for shipment overseas by C-5 Galaxy, in this particular case to Thailand. The aircraft is F-5E 79-1681. *Dave Thompkins*

The invasion that doomed South Vietnam began in January 1975 although the war of attrition had been going on even before the ceasefire two years before. Rarely did the SVNAF take the initiative and fight in the way it had been trained — but it was equally true that the economic state of the country did not allow the often extravagant deployment of firepower that the Americans could afford. Limits had already been placed on both fuel and armament stocks and some squadrons were disbanded.

The thrusts by the North brought the entire province of Phuoc Long into its grasp and created panic. The province was barely 50 miles from Saigon and its loss set up a chain reaction. The Air Force, faced as it was by intense AA fire from mobile guns accompanying any large concentration of enemy troops, could do little to prevent the panic that followed. Gradually South Vietnam's largest military asset — its air force — was nullified to the point of impotence. And as they moved forward the North Vietnamese threw a ring of AAA and SAMs around newly-won positions, secured their supply lines and waited for their next orders to move south.

A fundamental problem facing the SVNAF was the ground commanders' lack of understanding of airpower. High level discussions on strategy often did not include an Air Force representative, and military region commanders did not appreciate that air forces assigned to one region should have had the freedom to move to any threat area to be at all effective. A general lack of communications between the services compounded the difficulties. Low utilisation of what facilities there were also added to the situation, which rapidly became irredeemably chaotic.

With losses no longer being made good from the other side of the Pacific the SVNAF showed a marked reluctance to press home attacks. This attitude was worsened by poor intelligence, there being little air reconnaissance capacity on hand. The South Vietnamese lost four RF-5s before the offensive of 1975 began and in any event the camera fit was said to be incapable of providing the kind of detail required for accurate ground attack work. Film processing was also slow, using outdated equipment.

Nevertheless the SVNAF did continue to fly until the last weeks of its existence. By 14 March Ban Me Thot was in enemy hands and a general withdrawal was ordered. Realising that his reserves around Saigon were too weak to defend the capital, President Theiu ordered the army to pull back — leaving the air force with little choice but to do likewise, left as it was at Pleiku, which it was unable to defend. Next the entire Central Highlands were abandoned and the giant US base

and port of Da Nang quickly followed, along with other coastal cities which the Vietnamese command had hoped to defend effectively. All the time the NVA was openly travelling the roads and presenting numerous targets to air strikes. But the SVNAF could or would not press home attacks in the face of intensive defensive fire. Air attacks were invariably made 'above the flak' at altitudes of 10,000ft or above — too high for ordnance to have much effect. Starkly revealed was the failure of the US to provide aircraft that had the capability to survive in such a hostile environment.

The war had a matter of weeks to run; with enemy columns approaching the capital, nothing short of a miracle would save the country from defeat. The miracle did not happen. Instead there was a mass scramble to leave, as soldiers fought civilians to get aboard the last flights out of Vietnam.

The Air Force finally joined the exodus; there were ludicrous incidents such as an F-5 abandoned on the taxiway at Tan Son Nhut with its engines running; A-37s flown by renegade pilots bombing the Presidential palace and F-5s scrambling — too late — to catch them; Nguyen Cao Ky trying to marshal a small force of his F-5s to fly a last operation — against Phan Rang where the rebel A-37s had flown from — which never took place.

After the battle for Xuan Loc the main F-5 base at Bien Hoa had fallen and the remnants of the 23rd Wing pulled back to Tan Son Nhut. It was then estimated that the fighter force consisted of 109 F-5s and 169 A-37s, 93 of the former being operational. About 50% of the fighter force available for operations at the January 1973 ceasefire was on hand, there being 180 to defend Saigon — if it came to that. Some people thought the SVNAF was at last putting up a maximum effort as aircraft took off in the last days before the city surrendered. But the aircraft were heading not for the enemy lines, but refuge in Thailand, mostly to U-Tapao. Of 132 aircraft that arrived, there were 26 F-5s, comprising 22 E models and four As, as well as 27 A-37s.

The majority of these aircraft were whisked out of U-Tapao to the coast where they were lightered out to the US carrier *Midway*. The remnants of the SVNAF became deck storage for the voyage to Guam where the carrier docked on 11 May and unloaded 52 aircraft for onward transportation to the US. Even before *Midway* docked, the North Vietnamese were demanding compensation for these aircraft from the Thai government!

The F-5s that returned to the US were checked over and stored at McClellan AFB, pending sale abroad. In the event most remained in America to form the nucleus of aggressor training programmes for the Navy and Air Force; they joined 10 other

Top:
The first F-5F for Iran on a delivery test flight over the Mojave Desert. *via Hooks*

Above:
Serial number 75-0493 before delivery to the Royal Jordanian Air Force.

F-5Es embargoed from sale to Ethiopia, which too were operated by the American services.

The invading North Vietnames army discovered 87 abandoned F-5As and Bs, plus 27 E models, all of which were absorbed into their own air force to serve for a number of years. So ended the 'first phase' of the F-5's war service in South East Asia — but it was not to be the last time that the Tiger flew operational sorties in the area. Quite extensive use was apparently made of the aircraft when North Vietnam commenced hostilities with neighbouring Kampuchea. Reports quoted 'waves of F-5s' supporting the ground forces in the late 1978 invasion, and a year later nine Tigers were reportedly operating from Hanoi on interceptor duties as part of a composite squadron also equpped with the MiG-21F — an interesting combination considering the Tiger II's subsequent use by the US Navy and Air Force as a quasi MiG-21. The Hanoi unit is believed to have been joined by three other F-5/MiG-21 regiments formed after the end of the war in 1975.

Middle Eastern Service

Iran's modernisation programme included the F-5E, the first examples being delivered in August 1976 when 28 F-5Fs were received for conversion training. These two-seaters were followed by 141 F-5Es which were based at Mehrabad, Tabriz and Bushehr, equipping eight squadrons. The F-5Fs were initially supported by 22 F-5Bs, although by the time the first Tiger IIs arrived, Iran had disposed of virtually all its F-5As, mainly to Greece, Vietnam and Jordan.

Above:
Greenham Common IAT shows have brought many aircraft and air forces to the UK over the years, often on their only visit. These Jordanian F-5Es were present at IAT 1981. *Mod via Wheeler*

Above:
**RJAF No 1161 (the Western equivalent of the Arabic
numerals seen on the nose) taxies out during the 1981
IAT.** *MoD via Wheeler*

With an established inventory of F-5As and Bs,
the Royal Jordanian AF also acquired 55 F-5Es
and eight F-5Fs. These aircraft initially comple-
mented the existing aircraft in Nos 1 and 2
Squadrons but mainly were used to create three
more — Nos 9, 11 and 17 — based at Prince
Hassan AB, with an OCU at Mafraq for the
convenience of all the first-line units. The F-5Es
were used by Jordan primarily as interceptors,
carrying AIM-9Js on the wingtip stations, although
wing pylon and fuselage mounted stores were
fitted for secondary ground attack missions.

Where Tigers Rule
The build-up of the Tiger inventory in the South
Korean Air Force was paralleled by the initiation
of local manufacture and support by Hanjin
Corporation, utilising some facilities owned by
Korean Air Lines. By the early 1980s this
organisation had progressed to licence-assembly of
J85 engines. A milestone in Korea's association
with the F-5 took place on 9 September 1982 with
the first flight of a Hanjin F-5E powered by engines
assembled by Samsung Precision. By that time, the
Koreans had given the Tiger II a new name, the
not inappropriate Skymaster. The F-5E replaced
F-5As and F-5Bs in four squadrons, 126 of the
fighter version and nine F-5Fs, supported by 12
RF-5As, forming units of the 10th Tactical Fighter
Wing at Suwon.

Taiwan was put in an unenviable position when
the US recognised the People's Republic of China
in January 1979 and broke off diplomatic relations
with the Nationalist Government which had
received American military aid ever since World

War 2. By that time however the offshore island,
still publicly dedicated to the overthrow of the
Communist regime on the mainland, had established a viable aircraft industry and was producing
the F-5 under licences obtained from Northrop in
1973.

The People's Republic, said to be envious of its
tiny neighbour's ability to produce complex
modern combat aircraft, offered to pay the
equivalent cost of an F-5E (approximately $2.5
million), to any pilot willing to deliver one to the
mainland. The US government meanwhile faced
something of a dilemma over the future re-
equipment of its erstwhile ally in the increasingly
hostile atmosphere following recognition of Red
China. Taiwan continued to press for US
equipment, which led to some embarrassing
pontification by the US government.

There was for example the saga of the F-104
replacement; the Taiwanese wanted the F-4E
Phantom, but instead it was suggested that the
Americans could supply AIM-7 missiles to hang on
Taiwanese-assembled F-5Es. The F-5 has never
been cleared to carry the Sparrow AAM and
although the necessary modifications could
undoubtedly have been made, this would have
been a pointless exercise as such weapons would
have degraded the aircraft's performance to an
unacceptable level. The Nationalist Chinese
refused.

Northrop countered with a better offer in the
form of the new F-5G, the Tigershark forerunner,
which if necessary would have out-performed the
F-5E — particularly one carrying Sparrows. But
the US State Department vetoed this possibility,
reasoning that it could not be seen to be supplying
more sophisticated weapons to 'areas of potential
conflict' and instead offered the Hughes AGM-65
Maverick TV-guided missile system for Taiwan's
F-5E force. This combination, already developed

for Saudi Arabia's Tiger IIs, enabled a positive boost to the aircraft's firepower and is being adapted to F-5Es assembled by Aero Industry Development Centre at Taichung.

The already large Nationalist inventory of F-5As was increased by the number of F-5Es now being delivered and on order; at least 156 have been identified and the current requirement is believed to be for 187. AIDC has also received orders for 21 F-5Fs.

Units of the 1st Fighter Wing at Kuan Kuan now have a total of 70 F-5Es and a further 180 (a mix of old and current models) equip component squadrons of the 2nd and 3rd TFWs. The 5th Composite Wing is currently the operator of surviving T-38As, 30 examples of which were acquired under MAP.

In the current political wrangle between the

Above:
Four F-5Es, all ex-South Vietnam, with US-style serial presentation, in service with South Korea. *via Dorr*

Below:
The later camouflage scheme of ROKAF F-5Fs is similar to contemporary USAF interceptors — two shades of grey. *via Dorr*

USA, the People's Republic and Taiwan, military programmes come under close scrutiny. The Communist Chinese protested over an American offer to extend co-operative agreements on F-5E production — but at least implementation of this delayed a decision on the offshore regime's request for the F-16.

In the light of the unpredictable polices of the US, Taiwan took the decision to extend its own F-5E production, and allocate funds to its own R&D programme to build its own advanced fighter aircraft as an eventual replacement. In January 1982 the Nationalist Air Force had nine squadrons of F-5s, a total of 252 aircraft in A, E and F versions.

This understandably go-it-alone attitude of the Taiwanese is reflected in reports that the Air Force is engaged on an intensive training programme to overcome any potential threat from the mainland. Patrolling Nationalist fighters routinely intercept aircraft from the People's Republic over the Taiwan Strait which separates the two nations, as often as twice a week. The People's Republic aircraft usually turn away when the Nationalist interceptors arrive and there has not been a repeat of the incident several years ago when a mainland-based MiG-19 was shot down.

An April 1982 report in *Aviation Week* covered the activities of the F-5E-equipped 455th TFW at Chia Yi. Then commanded by Maj-Gen Hsu Ta-Mu, the wing comprised three F-5E/F fighter-bomber squadrons and an independent search and rescue squadron. One squadron of the wing was the 23rd led by Lt-Col Leo Wang. The wing conducted four to five combat air patrols a day over the Taiwan Strait, keeping close to the island's coastline facing the mainland. Operations included air support missions and escort to military provisioning flights to Kinmen, formerly Quemoy, nearer the mainland.

The 23rd Squadron's quick reaction alert scramble time was down to three minutes or less at the time of the report, a pair of F-5Es in camouflaged shelters at Chi Yi achieving a scramble in two minutes 58 seconds from alarm buzzer to take-off. The fighters were directed by a central air combat command post in Taipei equipped with a Hughes semi-automatic air defence radar that acquired and tracked multiple targets and passed information to the five fighter wings.

Right:
This fighter flight of Taiwanese F-5Es is of aircraft of one of the early production batches built by AIDC. *Hooks*

Below:
Among the countries to have adopted the low-visibility grey paint scheme is Taiwan. The F-5E is the backbone of that country's air defence against incursions into its airspace by Communist Chinese aircraft, and a quick reaction alert force is maintained around the clock. Chung Cheng F-5E is an AIDC-assembled machine, 77-0331. *via Dorr*

10 T-bird Talon

The year 1972 saw the last of 1,187 T-38s delivered to the USAF, by which time this remarkable trainer had been largely responsible for no less than 42,000 pilots of all nationalities gaining their coveted wings. The aircraft continued to provide good service and value for money and two years later the Talon was given a high 'seal of approval' by the USAF by being chosen as the new mount for the renowned 3600th Aerial Demonstration Squadron — the glamorous 'Thunderbirds'.

Selecting a trainer for the Thunderbirds was a radical departure from previous practice — the team had hitherto flown one of the Air Force's first-line fighters, beginning with the F-84 in May 1953 and culminating in the mighty F-4E Phantom in 1968. But six years later, the gas-guzzling Phantoms were becoming a little embarrassing in the fuel-conscious days of the early 1970s, and it would make sound economic sense — besides being good for USAF public relations — to change to an aircraft that was a little less expensive to operate.

The US Air Force was not alone in deciding to switch its premier aerobatic team to a trainer, although it was behind some of its counterparts in Europe, which had for years favoured trainers. Principal among these was the RAF Red Arrows, then mounted on the HS Gnat.

Nevertheless, considerable soul-searching went into the exercise before the Talon was confirmed; some saw the move as a retrograde one, feeling that the team was in some way losing its virile image. It had long been the boast of the USAF that the T-birds pilots were line pilots flying the self same type of aircraft as the operational squadrons in Tactical Air Command. True, they all had that certain extra something — perhaps a little more of the 'right stuff' than their squadron colleagues — but was a trainer right for the team? Then someone pointed out that the recruiting angle could be even better served by the T-38. While the would-be Air Force pilot at the front of an air show crowd *might* eventually get to join a Super Sabre, Thunderchief or Phantom squadron (depending on the year he saw the team perform) he would be *guaranteed* some T-38 time had he joined up any time after 1962. The fighter jocks were finally convinced.

By the early 1970s the USAF also had adequate T-38s in inventory following the wind-down of the requirement for high numbers of pilots to fulfil the SE Asia commitment. And while the PR boys had something of a hard time convincing the sceptics that four T-38s could be operated on the fuel load of just one F-4 while trying to forget the unforgettable experience of multiple J79s at full bore, the decision was taken. With hindsight it can be seen that the Thunderbirds' Talon period was tinged with cruel irony.

Considerable thought had to be given to making the T-38 as visible as possible, both through show routines, and colour scheme. Tiny in comparison with the Phantom, the Talon required an entirely new paint scheme, this being decided after a number of designs were submitted. Initially these centred on adapting the T-birds' striking black bird motif to the underside contours. But in this respect the Talon's superbly streamlined airframe went against it: the black bird, the thunderbird with its

Above:
The kind of precision formation for which the Thunderbirds are renowned. The Talon period was one of spectacular success and tragedy.

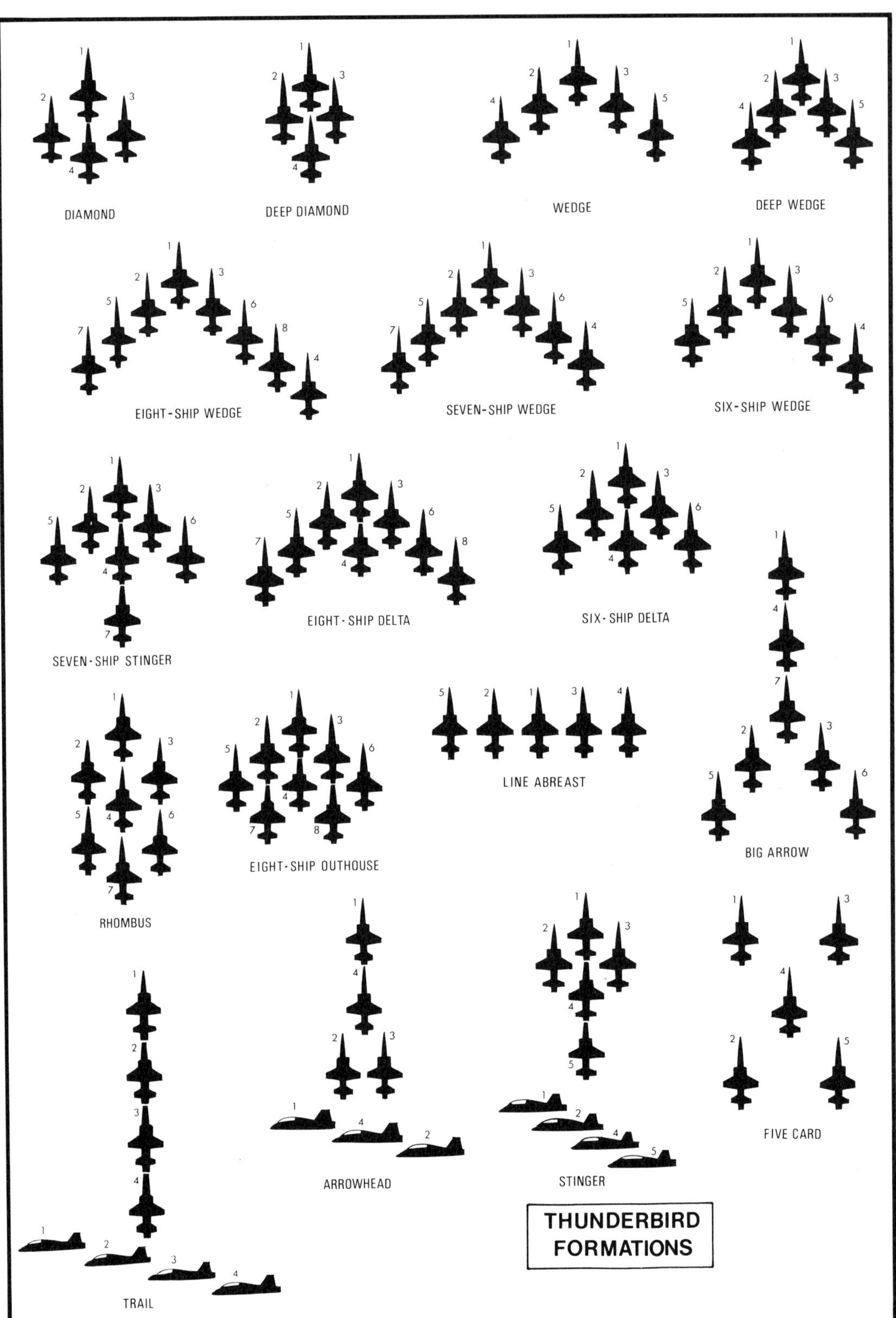

DIAMOND
DEEP DIAMOND
WEDGE
DEEP WEDGE
EIGHT-SHIP WEDGE
SEVEN-SHIP WEDGE
SIX-SHIP WEDGE
SEVEN-SHIP STINGER
EIGHT-SHIP DELTA
SIX-SHIP DELTA
RHOMBUS
EIGHT-SHIP OUTHOUSE
LINE ABREAST
BIG ARROW
TRAIL
ARROWHEAD
STINGER
FIVE CARD
THUNDERBIRD FORMATIONS

origins in North American Indian folklore, had to go.

Instead the Talon would have its lines enhanced by gracefully curved stripes on the fuselage and vertical tail. Under the wings would go a double arrowhead sweeping forward from the wingtips to sharpen even more the machine's needle nose. The team consequently achieved a good contrast between the top and lower surfaces when seen in plan, this becoming particularly evident during the fast rolls for which the T-38 was well known.

The Thunderbirds' graphics section, Northrop and fans all over the world contributed to the final design exhibited by the Talons; but as there was understandable reluctance to abandon the bird, they made some tests. Scale drawings of the motif, adapted to the Talon's cruciform shape, were examined from 1,500 scale feet, the average crowd-line to show-line distance. At that range the thunderbird certainly lost something — the T-38's wingspan was actually shorter than the wingspread of the motif applied to the underside of the F-4. Finally, tradition was shelved and the stripes and scallops painted on.

The size of the T-38 was to influence the team in other ways. Not being equipped for in-flight refuelling, the aircraft would be unlikely to be able to show the flag abroad unless they could be transported by air. This was apparently ruled out and the Thunderbirds looked forward to a busy 1974 season within the continental USA. Much thought also went into the show routines, the demonstration team manager having to ensure that the small aircraft was not lost to view at any time during a display. But what the Talon lacked in size and thrilling brute power it more than made up for in grace and manoeuvrability, and for 1974, the team reintroduced a 'behind the crowd' opening pass. Between March and November (the usual 10-month season) the team honed its act with the new aircraft.

The Talon's slick flight characteristics also enabled a return to a second solo aircraft, which the T-birds had not used for seven years. This crowd stopper was first flown in Talons in 1976 (America's bicentennial year) dropped for 1977 and 1978, and permanently reinstated in 1979. The maximum number of T-38s the Thunderbirds flew was eight, 'wedge' 'delta' and 'outhouse' being the big formations employed for this number of aircraft. At most shows, however, the USAF demonstration squadron uses five or six aircraft for the majority of its formation aerobatics, each pilot flying his aircraft as one with the leader. Other aircraft are held in reserve or fly solo positions.

Another slight but significant change to T-bird tradition with the advent of the little trainer was the disappearance of the black tail of the slot pilot's aircraft. This feature had over the years become more or less standard due to the sooty emissions from the big engines that powered most of the team's previous mounts. So common did it become that the sooty vertical surfaces were finally painted — black. But it was not so with the Talon. The little twin J85s were not smokers and consequently this feature was not part of the Talon period, 1974 to 1981.

The 1981 season closed in September, 11 weeks short. It had been a bad year for the team. On 9 May the opposing solo pilot was killed when his T-38 crashed inverted at Hill AFB, Utah. The aircraft came down just outside the air base apparently with both engines stopped. On 8 September a second T-bird Talon went in at Cleveland Airport, Ohio. Taking off after completing the show, team leader Lt-Col David Smith had a multiple birdstrike when he ran into a flock of seagulls. Smith and his groundcrew passenger ejected at low altitude but Smith's parachute failed to open in time. His groundcrewman survived having suffered only minor injuries. Worse — far worse — was to come.

On the morning of 10 January 1982 the four 'diamond' aircraft formation aircraft (Nos 1-4) climbed out of Nellis en route to Indian Springs and more practice. *None* of them would return. Approximately 30 minutes later four Talons lay shattered on the floor of the Nevada desert, their quartet of pilots dead in the wreckage of their aircraft. The 1982 show season was cancelled before it had even begun.

Witnesses stated that the aircraft flew into the ground from a line-abreast loop. As they flattened out the stabiliser of Maj Norman Lowry's aircraft jammed, forcing it into a terminal dive. The T-38s did not have radios and the other three pilots, Capt Willie Mays (number two), Joseph 'Pete' Peterson (three) and Mark Melacon (slot) apparently noticed nothing until it was too late. Examination of the crash site indicated that Lowry impacted first, followed by No 4. Numbers 2 and 3 hit last.

There was a subsequent suggestion that had a voice-actuated radio circuit been installed Maj Lowry might have had time to warn the others to effect their recovery. Lowry himself apparently had no time to make hand signals, being fully occupied in trying to pull the T-38 out of its dive with both hands on the stick. He probably would not have realised his dive was critical until the last few seconds, by which time it was too late. There was so little time; all three pilots would have had their eyes on the leader's aircraft and the 100ft planned exit height from the loop would have been lost very quickly indeed.

The Thunderbirds are no strangers to tragedy

but this, the worst in its history, was particularly so considering the Talon's excellent safety record. Maj Lowry had only been the leader for some three months, having replaced David Smith the previous October.

The first two crashes brought forth demands that the team be disbanded and the second multiple loss brought the Thunderbirds to the brink once more. These pressures were resisted but the Talon period was over. It was ironic that the same aircraft that had trained thousands of pilots should have ended a highlight of its career in this fashion, but few students ever flew the T-38 anywhere near the limits required of the Thunderbirds virtually every time they take off.

Except for one show in Puerto Rico, the Thunderbirds' Talons were not seen outside the US, but the thousands who witnessed over 400 shows by the diminutive White Rocket can attest to the fact that it was one of the most attractive aircraft ever used. A total of 12 T-38As were acquired for the team's use, including back up and support aircraft. They carried the team through their most challenging season, that of bicentennial year 1976 when record crowds watched every show. The celebrations marking America's 200 years of existence introduced a variation in the T-birds' tail marking, the large black numbers being replaced by the bicentennial 'pretzel' device.

Not before 2 April 1983 did the Thunderbirds again perform in public. Their 2,457th show was the first with the F-16 — the team was back on a fighter. But the T-38 remains into the Fighting Falcon era as part of the entourage that accompanies the T-birds wherever they go, two aircraft playing a supporting role. Further evidence of the earlier period greets the visitor to the team's base area at Nellis, where a T-38 stands as a permanent memorial, resplendent in the team's colours.

An illuminating account of a Thunderbird pilot's routine was written in 1976 by Capt Gil Mook, a member of the team from October 1973 to January 1976. It well showed the pressures as well as the pride that comes with a posting to a unit which simply stated, has a mission to 'Plan and present precision aerial manoeuvres'.

Gil Mook was 17 when he first saw the Thunderbirds perform in F-100 Super Sabres on Memorial Day, 1960. The team's show at Andrews AFB affected him in 'a most unusual way' although he then knew nothing about the intricacies of flying high-performance aircraft in formation. But the bug had bitten:

'Thirteen years later I signed in at an Air Force station whose hangar was marked with a red, white and blue sign reading "Home of the USAF Thunderbirds"'.

'As a fighter pilot schooled in fighter tactics, I learned quickly that my tour here would be much more than flying. It would not be easy, nor would it be without its moments of pride and achievements. I also quickly learned that while it is true the pilots have the squadron's most glamorous role, without the constant and complete support of the Thunderbird maintenance and support people, the team would not exist as a viable organisation.

'The Thunderbird squadron is comprised 75 members, 10 officers and 65 enlisted men. The officers consist of seven pilots, an executive support officer, an information officer and a maintenance officer. The enlisted men are all NCOs who together comprise a spectrum of 25 different career fields, ranging from a full complement of crew chiefs and maintenance technicians to administrative, supply and information specialists.

'Each Thunderbird NCO is outstanding in his career field and each of the coveted team positions is competed for by as many as 100 applicants. Once a man arrives, he is put on 30-day probation, during which he is under continuous evaluation to make sure that he can maintain the high Thunderbird standards. Only after successfully completing this rigorous period is he brought before a council of Thunderbird NCOs and given his patch. Even after successfully surviving this test, the coveted patch must be considered "on loan" because if he ever fails to meet the high standards expected of him or if he fails to favourably represent the Air Force, he will be asked to resign from the team.

'A great deal of time and effort is devoted to the pilot selection process. Each applicant is carefully screened by every Thunderbird pilot and a selection made of approximately 15 'semi-finalists'.

Above:
'V' formation with little space between aircraft.

80

Each one makes one deployment with the team so that he may become familiar with its operation and give team members an equal opportunity to evaluate him as a potential Thunderbird. After the semi-finalists have all travelled with the team, we then meet to discuss our impressions and select five or six finalists.

'The finalists travel to Nellis as a group and each man will fly a Thunderbird aircraft in formation from the back seat. Incidentally there is no requirement for the finalist to be current in the aircraft and oddly enough, there is no advantage if he is. The ride consists of a formation take-off, some wing work, rejoins, and several aerobatic flight manoeuvres. The flight is extremely demanding and designed to thoroughly tax the applicant's flying ability. In evaluating a man's performance, we are not looking for a demonstration of precision formation flying — rather we are taking a good look at the man's basic flying skills and, perhaps most important, his air sense. Once again we sit down and evaluate the final applicants and send our recommendations to a board of senior officers for their final selection.

'The most demanding part of the year for the entire team is the training season, which takes place in January and February. It was during this season that I learned just how physically demanding flying with the Thunderbirds can be. The completion of each training mission is marked by an aching arm and a sweat-drenched flying suit.'

Syllabus Progress
'The flying training syllabus is an orderly progression of missions that starts from basic two-ship flights in formation and continues through to the entire show sequence. As a diamond pilot, I began by learning the basics of flying precision formations and, most importantly, developing a high degree of confidence in the leader. Maximum performance formation take-offs, lazy eights, whifferdills, easy wing rolls, and trail formations are all practised, starting with what we call a "spread formation", which is 4ft of wing tip clearance. Slowly, proficiency improves, and we start to work into the normal diamond formation. Morning and afternoon, day in and day out, over and over, the manoeuvres are practised. As expertise is gained, the missions expand to three and then four-ship formations.

'After a certain proficiency level has been reached, we start working closer to the ground and our training area moves from a dry lake bed north of Nellis to Indian Springs auxiliary airfield where the show is put together with the solo and honed to a fine edge. While we diamond pilots, or "drones" as the solo pilot calls us, are practising our formation manoeuvres, the solo pilot is rehearsing his bone-rattling series of manoeuvres.

'While putting the final touches on our show routine at Indian Springs, we are constantly performing before our severest critics — ourselves. All training is observed and evaluated by a pilot in a chase aircraft and a videotape recording of each mission is shot from a simulated show centre on the ground. Use of the videotape recorder (VTR) greatly enhances the effectiveness of our flight debriefing and the safety of our operation. The VTR lets us view the air show from the spectator's standpoint and to adjust our aircraft alignment so that we look optically symmetrical from the ground. For example it is actually necessary to fly 'out of position' during some of our diamond manoeuvres so that when viewed from the ground the formation will look symmetrical.'

Below:
Closing it up a bit for a wingtip separation of only a few feet.

High Tempo

A typical training day begins with an 07.30 briefing for the morning training mission. The tempo of the missions starts with a 'time hack', followed immediately by the Logistics Officer's report on the maintenance status of the aircraft. The leader (Boss) then reviews in detail each manoeuvre to be flown, discussing any problem that anyone might be having. Special emphasis is always placed on absolute consistency of procedures, including exact wording for all the required radio calls. Every time we go out and fly, whether it is a deployment, a practice, or an air show, the basic procedures are exactly the same.

'As soon as the briefing is over it is time to hustle outside and get into the jets. Walking out to your aircraft, you try to recall all the techniques that you can use to improve your flying. Taxying out on the active runway you prepare for the first flying task, the formation take-off.

'The Thunderbird formation take-off is considerably different from a standard fighter wing take-off; aside from being closer together, the difference is the aircraft is actually pulled off the runway with excess flying speed, which enables you to manoeuvre precisely to your position. As you accelerate down the runway, the Boss will call "nosewheels" which is the cue to pull sharply aft on the stick. As you pull your jet into the air, you raise the landing gear as soon as the struts extend and move to your correct position. The nose keeps coming up to 60° nose high and then a fairly rapid roll-off begins, which completes the maximum performance take-off. We then fly the eight-minute hop to Indian Springs and start into the show sequence.

'Starting with the Diamond Roll and into Trail Roll, the mission rapidly progresses to the point where you are counting the manoeuvres to be flown, so your aching arm can get some relief. During the practice mission you are working and concentrating so hard that you lose all sense of time. After what seems like about 10 seconds, the 30-minute show sequence is over and you are flying back to Nellis to pitch up and land.

'During the trip back, your mind is mulling over the flight and you hope that through some miracle the all-seeing VTR didn't see you louse up a manoeuvre. As you climb out and head for debriefing, your flying suit is completely soaked and you are convinced that your arm has been rendered totally useless.

'Our debriefings are very thorough and cover every aspect of the mission. Every manoeuvre is discussed in detail, with constant reference to the

Below:
Slight variation in markings is obvious in this view, with the flags of countries visited replacing the T-bird badge under the second cockpit. Capt Gil Mook is flying No 2.

video playback. No one is immune to criticism and after a few debriefings you learn that being a member of the Thunderbirds is no job for the "thin-skinned".

'And so it goes on, until the first part of March rolls round and it is finally time to hit the road and find out just how good you really are. Completion of the training season does not produce a high plateau of proficiency that will remain with you the entire season. On the contrary, we must fly frequently to maintain and improve our skills and we notice ourselves losing that fine edge if we go more than three or four days without flying.

'The show season begins after the schedule is approved in early December; the preparation machinery then goes into action to ensure that all the details essential to a smooth running and professional operation are covered. Every man on the team is charged with ensuring that his particular area of responsibility is co-ordinated with the rest. In flying an average 100 demonstrations a year, we cannot afford the luxury of slack days for smoothing out the wrinkles of a show site. The success of the operation depends on every man knowing his job — if an aircraft encounters mechanical problems, the maintenance crew have to be prepared to work around the clock to fix it.'

Showtime
'All the hard training and preparations are over when seven jets and our C-130 support aircraft are airborne and heading for the first air show. The formation joins up and the Boss tells us to go "spread". We slide out to maintain exactly 4ft of wingtip clearance and press on to our destination. As you fly you reflect on all the hard work. Somehow it seems hard to believe that you are now going to do the real thing in front of thousands of people.

'We plan our fuel management to ensure that we have enough left for some arrival manoeuvres. These serve three purposes: first they help maintain our proficiency; second they allow us to get the "lie of the land" and third, they serve as an advance advertisement for the show. At precisely the appointed time, we make our opening pass and set up for the arrival. During these manoeuvres we catch glimpses of the surrounding terrain and it comes as no small surprise that we are no longer over the bleak desert of Indian Springs.

'After landing we greet the press, the sponsors and the show organisers; at briefing we run the video again and the team narrator brings us up to date on any changes to our itinerary. The next order of business is to survey the show site from a light aircraft to ensure there are no obstacles that might affect the show.

'The next day is ushered in by the persistent ring of an alarm clock and the butterflies in your stomach and sweaty palms tell you that the big show day has finally arrived. After arriving at the show there is time to kill before the briefing, which turns out to be the same skull session that we have on every mission we fly. After the briefing is over, the walk through the crowd is like walking down a long, deserted road. The one thought in your mind is flying a good show. Your stomach butterflies are doing maximum performance rolls and the adrenalin is beginning to flow. After waiting for what seems an eternity it is finally time to march out to the aircraft and go fly. We start the jets, go through the checks and taxi out to the runway, using the same procedures we use on all our flights. Once on the runway, a final inspection is completed and the Boss calls "Let's run 'em up". I place my hands on my knees to damp out the shaking as I hold the brakes.

'At last we are airborne. The "roll off" after the maximum performance take-off sheds all the nerviness and you become a machine that runs on hours of hard training and the mutual trust that prevails throughout the show routine. Then just as fast as it began, the show is over. Taxying in, your emotions begin the unwinding process and you have a few moments to reflect on your performance. If it was a good show, you are filled with a warm glow of satisfaction. If it was not as good as it should have been, a gnawing sense of dissatisfaction eats at your insides and manifests itself as a burning desire to get airborne again and do a better job.

'After meeting the crowd and signing autographs it feels great to sit down at the briefing and continue to unwind as you listen to the comments of the Thunderbird Logistics Officer who serves as the safety observer and grader during the show. We receive a grade on everything, starting with our marching to the aircraft, taxying, take-off, the entire show, and landing. Every possible facet of the show is discussed and reviewed through the "instant replay" system of the VTR. Every mistake in a manoeuvre takes points away and the grading is received. It takes a practised eye to objectively grade our performance and I can assure you that our grader has never been mistaken for Santa Claus.

'Later that day, after the various functions scheduled for the evening, you finally hit the sack. Your exhausted body tells you that you have earned your Air Force pay for the day. Just before the blackout of deep sleep takes over, you remember that the next day brings another deployment. And on and on it will go for nine long months. Nine months of the most demanding and yet the most fantastic job I can imagine.'

11 Supermart Tigers

On 5 June 1973 Richard Nixon sanctioned renewed arms sales to South America thereby reversing the policies of previous US administrations. There were still some constraints on certain weapons Third World countries were allowed to buy in order to maintain some balance of power in the region but the move generally opened the door to US manufacturers which had seen a gradual shift away from their own products to those of European countries. The sale of Mirages to Peru in 1968 put supersonic combat aircraft into the hands of a Latin American power for the first time and it was clear that the US had a potentially large market on its own doorstep — one that it was in danger of losing.

One of the first countries to take advantage of the new American policy was Brazil, which as far back as 1966 had showed interest in the F-5 although embargoes had prevented any deal being struck. The State Department allowed Northrop to re-open negotiations in 1974 and in October these bore fruit when the Brazilian Government signed a $72.3 million contract for 36 F-5Es and six F-5Bs. In common with a number of other countries, the Brazilian F-5Es had an additional dorsal fin fillet to improve directional stability and VHF blade aerials just aft of the cockpit.

Equipping two of the FAB's most famous fighter squadrons, 1° and 2° Esqudrao in the 1st Fighter Group, the F-5Es are based at Santa Cruz near Rio. In addition, a third squadron operates from Canoas, Porto A'legre. Air interception duties are interspersed with air-to-air refuelling sorties using two KC-130H tankers, the Brazilian Tiger IIs having starboard-side refuelling probes fitted as required. Standard air intercept armament is guns and AIM-9J Sidewinders AAMs on wingtip stations.

The 1st FG now has its own hangars at Santa Cruz but until recently the F-5Es and all other aircraft on the base, including an AT-26 Xavante unit, Navy S-2 Trackers and a UH-1H squadron, were comfortably accommodated in a giant Zeppelin shed built in 1934. This still dominates the Santa Cruz base.

Chile also took advantage of the lifting of the USA arms embargo, ordering 15 F-5Es and three F-5Fs shortly before the Marxist government of President Allende was deposed. The Chileans wanted the F-5 to update the Hunter interceptor force which had been established after F-5As were refused in 1967; despite the military coup, Northrop was able to fulfil the $40 million order.

Deliveries began in June 1976, the F-5E being favoured over the MiG-21 being pressed on Chile by the Soviet Union. The FAC's aircraft, which also feature the dorsal fin extension and VHF blade aerial, now equip Grupo 7 at Antofagasta on the south Atlantic coast.

Talks between the Kenyan minister of defence and his US counterparts in June 1976 led to one of the largest orders ever placed with a newly-independent African state. Negotiations resulted in a $5 million credit, it being understood by the US that the Kenyans would buy ex-Iranian F-5As. In fact the Kenyan Air Force required a full squadron of F-5Es, plus trainers. Ten E models and four F-5Fs were duly delivered as part of a $75 million order which included spares and Sidewinder AAMs. They are currently based at Nanyuki and give Kenya's '82 Air Force (to give its present name) an interceptor capability for the first time in its history, and some counter to the possible threat posed by the predominantly Chinese and Russian inventories of its neighbours.

The F-5E also became the principal combat aircraft of the Indonesia air arm under a re-equipment programme started in the early 1980s. Acquisition of 12 F-5Es and four F-5Fs was completed by 1982.

Singapore's F-5E inventory has now reached at least 24 with more on order; six F-5Fs are in service, three having been delivered in 1979 as part of a batch which included the bulk of the F-5Es, 21 aircraft. These equip No 144 Squadron at Tengah, an interceptor unit which also undertakes conversion training with the two-seaters. The F-5Es use the AIM-9J as their primary AAM armament.

Malaysia was the 'launch customer' for the RF-5E TigerEye, two examples of which were delivered as part of the Perista expansion programme. This reconnaissance capability boosted current RMAF F-5s to 20 aircraft, there currently being 14 F-5Es and four F-5Fs, two of the E models of the original 15 delivered having been written off; one was replaced in April 1981. No 12 (Lightning) Squadron at Butterworth is the Malaysian F-5 unit, the F model trainers having replaced two F-5Bs which were passed to the Royal Thai Air Force.

The continuing conflict in neighbouring Vietnam

Below left:
One of Brazil's F-5Es on an early test flight. *via Dorr*

Bottom left:
The first of Brazil's F-5Es was No 4820, ex-74-1582, seen here climbing out of Palmdale on flight test. Brazil was one of the countries that stipulated the dorsal fin extension.

Top:
Chile became an F-5E customer in June 1978, the air force's Grupo 7 operating both variants. J-804 was ex-75-0446. *Northrop via Dorr*

Below:
Kenya's $75 million order for F-5Es and associated equipment was a big surprise to Northrop, the company having assumed that that air force would adopt far cheaper F-5As. This is one of the early production aircraft in US grey scheme prior to a darker camouflage scheme being adopted by Kenya. *via Hooks*

Top:
Singapore based its combat aircraft update programme on the F-5E and A-4 Skyhawk. No 144 Squadron at Tengah is the F-5 unit, with both E and F models. F-5F No 850 (ex-77-0359) and F-5E No 800 were the initial deliveries of each version. *via Dorr*

Above:
Malaysia was the first country to order the RF-5E, the first aircraft of 10 delivered being seen here on flight test. 'TUDM' on the fin stands for Tentera Udara Diraja Malaysia and 'M29' is the current Malaysian type number for the F-5 which used to be M22. Designations and national markings were revised during the 1981-85 five-year plan. *via Dorr*

Below:
Wearing the pre-1982 square national insignia, FM-2204 was the second F-5E delivered to the Royal Malaysian Air Force for No 12 Squadron at Butterworth. Its MAP serial was 74-1447. *via Hooks*

and Kampuchea obliged Thailand to boost its
defence forces to protect its border areas and in
1976 a $50 million order for 17 F-5Es and three
F-5Fs heralded the start of a modernisation
programme that continues into the present decade.

Although no longer eligible for US aid under
MAP after 1978, Thailand's orders for military
equipment are still largely directed towards the
US. By 1980, follow-on orders for the Tiger II
enabled the formation of a second 1st Wing unit,
the 102nd Squadron, at Nakhom Ratchasima. The
current inventory is 40 F-5Es, six F-5Fs and 24
RF-5Es, these machines apparently being divided
between the 102nd and 104th Squadrons, the latter
in the 4th Wing at Takhli.

One of the most recent F-5 customers is the
Sudanese Air Force, which received 10 Tiger IIs
and two F-5Fs primarily to deter aggressive moves
by Libya. These aircraft were supplied under
favourable terms by the US, Sudan being
financially unable to take up a 1978 option to
purchase 16 Mirage 5s and ordering F-5s instead.

Financial difficulties also prevented Tunisia
adding significantly to its combat capability before
1983 when a modest five-year modernisation plan
was announced. Part of this was an order for six
F-5Es and two F-5Fs, urgently needed to boost the
tiny force of eight MB 326 fighter-bombers.
Deliveries were due to be completed in 1985 in a
$200 million deal.

An agreement made with King Feisal of Saudi
Arabia in 1972 resulted in a series of orders for the
F/RF-5E, F and B under a large-scale modernisation plan by one of the richest and most influential
countries in the Middle East. The Saudis have also
financed developments of the F-5's capability

tailored to their own requirements, and it is true to
say that these aircraft are among the most potent
of the entire series, with a weapons delivery
capability superior to that of most other air arms
equipped with Tiger IIs.

Initial contracts were placed with Northrop
under a $130 million agreement signed in 1971,
with first deliveries of 20 F-5Bs taking place in
early 1973. The first F-5E was delivered the
following year, 30 aircraft having been ordered in
the autumn of 1973. Further deliveries were then
curtailed by the brief oil embargo on the US by
Arab countries, but in 1975 Saudi Arabia signed
for 40 more F-5Es and 20 F-5Fs. This $750 million
contract also covered a research and development
programme to equip the F-5E to carry the Hughes
AGM-65A Maverick missile and its laser guidance
system and provided for Northrop to furnish initial
technical support and spares as well as pilot and
technician training, with the Saudis paying for the
hardware.

RSAF F-5Es were also fitted with the Litton
LN-33 inertial navigation system, in-flight refuelling probes and the capability to deliver laser-
guided 'smart' bombs. Radar warning was
provided, as was ECM capability based on
frequency agility; the two-seaters had canopy
mounted Northrop AVQ-27 manual laser target
designators.

The Saudis' traditional role in maintaining the
balance of power in the Arab world by exerting
influence on their neighbours was highlighted
during the re-equipment of the Egyptian Air Force
following the peace treaty with Israel in October
1973. As Egypt gradually built an inventory based
on Western aircraft rather than Russian, its
shopping list included the F-5E and F, a batch of
50 being ordered in 1977. Egypt still relied heavily
on Saudi financial assistance for such purchases
and despite the fact that the EAF then had far
greater combat capability in the form of Mirages
and MiG-23s, the Saudis withdrew funding for the
F-5E.

Purchases of F-5Es by the Saudis continues into
the present decade; the E and F models are being
delivered in various batches and 70 E models and
24 F-5Fs are known to have been delivered under
the 'Peace Hawk' programme. This joint agreement with the US, which involves flying new
aircraft to the customer via various staging points
rather than transporting them, currently includes
follow-on orders for the RF-5E TigerEye. Ten of
these reconnaissance models are already in service
with the RSAF and have presumably replaced
examples of the F-5E which were apparently
equipped with the early, F-5A-type camera nose,
some of which were specified when the Tiger II
was originally ordered. In 1985 'Peace Hawk'

Above:
Saudi Arabia also ordered a number of RF-5Es, early models which adopted the RF-5A nose section before availability of the 'long nose' version. *via Hooks*

brought four RF-5Es for Saudi Arabia (one incidentally in an all-matt black colour scheme) into Prestwick, Scotland, on 13-14 January.

'Peace Hawk's' phased deliveries include support, services and training provision by the US, as well as weapons. The F-5Es use the AIM-9, 850 of which have been delivered out of the 1,000 requested, and the Hughes Maverick, the Saudis being allowed 650 missiles of this type although they requested 2,500. The AGM-65A is carried singly by the F-5E on a special lightweight launcher designed specifically for the aircraft, it being found that the US triple-round installation was too heavy, reduced ground clearance and produced too much drag. Saudi Arabia funded the development and production of this launcher for the F-5E and is understood to have ordered the Matra R.550 Magic AAM for both the F-5E and F. The DoD offered the Saudis 1,600 AGM-65Bs in the spring of 1984, the quoted order value including nine load training missiles with spares, equipment and logistical support, being $119 million. This was apparently in response to a Saudi request to provide its F-5E force with 'a full 60-day war stock' of Mavericks for an anti-armour role.

RSAF Tiger IIs equip No 7 Squadron at Dharhan, No 3 at Taif and No 10 at Khamis Mushayt. The F-5Bs equip No 15 Squadron which shares Dharhan with No 7's F-5Fs.

The first moves to sell the F-5E to Switzerland took place in late 1974 with a recommendation of the merits of the aircraft made to parliament by Defence Minister Rudolf Gnaegi. The Swiss requested formal letters of offer from the US Department of Defense confirming that Switzerland would participate in manufacture. This was agreed and early in 1975 Northrop took 70-1386, the second production F-5E, to Switzerland for an extensive six-week evaluation against competing Mirages.

The Swiss Air Force (Flugwaffe) needed a replacement aircraft for the venerable DH Venom FB 50 fighter-bomber which at that time equipped no less that nine squadrons. It was also intended that the new aircraft would allow some reduction in the inventory of Hawker Hunter interceptors.

Accompanied by a second F-5E (71-1421), Northrop directed an intensive flying programme — 60 sorties of all types in one of the most demanding environments in the world. The Flugwaffe has an enviable reputation for operating high performance aircraft in defence of Switzerland's airspace with an elan rarely matched anywhere in the world. The predominantly conscript (militia) force is well used to flying from air bases situated near mountain ranges, and the high, thin air conditions present few problems. Exercises frequently include flying *through* the mountain passes and good manoeuvrability is an essential asset in any combat aircraft the Swiss operate.

Originally the Swiss sought a number of changes in the F-5E to better tailor it to their operating conditions, including revision of flap travel, installation of ILS to enable steeper approaches, and also local airframe stengthening to allow fully loaded aircraft to be slung from hoists and lifted up to hangar roofs. In October 1975 the Swiss cabinet made a formal request to parliament for the purchase of 72 F-5s, 66 E model fighters and six F-5F trainers.

The Swiss arranged for the first 13 F-5Es and all six F-5Fs to be delivered from MAP stocks, with the balance of 53 being assembled by the Federal

Above:

A Swiss Air Force F-5E being towed out at Palmdale ready for disassembly, loading on to an eight pack and flight delivery. The F-5 delivery of 19 Northrop-built aircraft saw the first landing of a C-5 Galaxy in Switzerland. The machine shown was the ninth aircraft to be completed, ex-76-1534.

Above right:

No 3,000 of the T-38/F-5 production run pictured at Palmdale prior to delivery to Saudi Arabia. In the background is one of the F-5Es destined for Chile.

Aircraft Factory at Emmen. Programme cost was put at $450 million, unit cost being $3.85 million including spares. The total aircraft cost was put at $277 million with the remainder going on armament, infrastructure and logistics support.

With an additional cost of $181,000 per aircraft added to cover final assembly in Switzerland, this particular F-5E programme was by no means cheap. Consequently the additional requirements were reduced to two, the fitting of larger diameter wheels to accommodate larger brakes and substituting the liquid oxygen system for a gaseous system.

The first public view of a Swiss F-5E was on 25 August 1979 when Dubendorf Air Base held an open day, aircraft J-3021 (76-1546) being part of the display. By that time, the deployment of the F-5E in the Flugwaffe had been slightly changed in that it would be used mainly as fighter cover for the Hunters which were to undertake a ground attack role, while the Mirage III remained as the high altitude interceptor type. Some Venoms were also retained for some time after the F-5E entered service.

Initial operating units were Fliegerstaffeln 8, 11,18 and 19, all of which had at least one F-5F for conversion training. That the F-5E was very quickly absorbed by the Flugwaffe was shown on 17 May 1979 when the 1,000th flight by an F-5E was celebrated. First Lt Jurg Witschi made the milestone sortie and naturally joined in the celebration at Payerne.

That the F-5 has been Northrop's most successful aerospace programme in the company's history is hardly in doubt; in one year alone (1975) sales brought a net income of $18.13 million, a result then comparable with only one other US aerospace firm in the top 12 offering a single main product. This was LTV (as it then was) which took the bulk of its business solely from sales of the A-7. In October that year the operational availability of the world F-5E fleet was put at 82% and according to operators' figures the average monthly use of the aircraft was 22 hours, the total number of hours flown worldwide being 38,000. Production at Hawthorne had then reached 18 aircraft a month.

On 9 December 1976 Northrop delivered the 3,000th example of the T-38/F-5 line, an F-5E for Saudi Arabia. The company held a ceremony attended by some 10,000 people to mark to occasion. Guests included Gen William J. Evans, commander of USAF Systems Command, who put Northrop's production record into perspective by saying:

'The Air Force is grateful when an airplane comes along that offers both high performance and economy, as well as long life. It isn't every day that the United States Air Force is party to a production run of that size. In fact, you would have to add up our procurements for every year back to 1968 to come up with a total of 3,000. And that's not just counting one type — its all the aircraft we've bought for the last nine years'.

12 Make Like a MiG

Towards the end of the US involvement in Vietnam, statistics revealed that the kill ratio of US Air Force and Navy fighters over the interceptors of the North Vietnamese Air Force were less than impressive — they barely averaged more than 2:1 for some engagements. This ratio was nowhere near as high as that of Korea (a war with certain similarities to Vietnam) which returned an air superiority figure of approximately 10:1 in the Americans' favour. And although the operational environment of South East Asia was in many ways unique, the fact remained that the achievements in air-to-air combat were very poor. It was not that there was anything intrinsically wrong with American fighters — they were on some counts significantly superior to their adversaries — but the fault was seen to lie in pilot training. Crews simply had not been taught to get the best out of their aircraft.

It was therefore decided that both the Navy and the Air Force would instigate training programmes to ensure that never again would such a situation be allowed to develop. In any future conventional conflict American fighter pilots would, if humanly possible, come out on top. Under the old maxim 'know your enemy' the services would raise air combat training to top priority, not simply by pitting their first line aircraft against each other, but by introducing a type more representative of the Soviet-bloc types US air forces had met, and presumably would continue to meet, over a battlefield.

Flown by pilots who would plan, fly and fight like Warsaw Pact air arms, this 'enemy' force would, it was reckoned, make extreme demands on line squadrons pitted against them. It was a unique concept in military tactics — have aircraft flown by Americans but in all other respects react like the 'other side'.

During investigations into this plan, it was obvious that potentially the most dangerous aircraft in the North Vietnamese inventory had been the MiG-21; even though more combat had taken place against the MiG-17, its obsolescence made it unrepresentative in the 1980s and 1990s. The MiG-21 was therefore the yardstick, the one to beat. This extremely able type had also been met in combat by friendly nations in the Middle East — particularly Israel — and the salient features of it, particularly small size in comparison to contemporary Air Force and Navy fighters, should ideally be matched as closely as possible. Only the T-38/F-5 series came anywhere close on that score and other similarities were found in US

evaluation of the MiG-21. Although not quite in the same performance class, the T-38 was the only aircraft available when the new air combat manoeuvring training programme was started.

The US Navy was the first to highlight the lack of realistic air combat training and in 1969 ordered six T-38As for evaluation as a suitable 'aggressor' aircraft. That title would subsequently be taken up and 'used in anger' by the USAF, although to the Navy this training meant a stint with the Fighter Weapons Wing school of air warfare, at Miramar, California.

Studies into how to improve air combat capability throughout the fleet fighter force began with a report commissioned by Naval Air Systems Command's Capt Frank W. Ault. He set out to examine all aspects of Naval fighter engagements in Vietnam. Among other things, the Ault Report recommended establishing a nucleus of specialists who could pass on their skills to fleet pilots.

Under the auspices of the Fighter Weapons Wing the T-38s and a number of A-4 Skyhawks (which satisfactorily 'doubled' for the MiG-17) were employed. But the Ault Report initially recommended the establishment of suitable areas over which to conduct this form of training, as well as instrumentation to track participating aircraft via unmanned solar-powered stations slaved to control and display stations. This ACMR — Air Combat Maneuvering Range — was the subject of a contract on 4 May 1971, for an ACMR to be built at MCAS Yuma. It was declared operational in December 1973. A second range was contracted for in October 1974, this being located at Kitty Hawk, SC and under the jurisdiction of NAS Oceana. A third, joint-service, ACMR was established at Langley AFB.

Under the subsequent memorandum of agreement between the Navy and Air Force (which calls the system Air Combat Maneuvering Instrumentation), ranges were established at Nellis and Tyndall AFBs, Florida. To accommodate aggressor training overseas, similar facilities were provided in Sardinia and the Philippines.

A typical range covers more than 700sq miles and has four major sub-systems. The Aircraft Instrumentation Subsystem (AIS) is housed in a pod and mounted on a standard weapons pylon (invariably the wingtip station on the F-5) and electrically interfaced with the aircraft's weapons system. This pod continually measures inflight air pressures and converts these to AOA, angle of sideslip, airspeed and Mach number data. It also furnishes weapons data and firing functions to the pilot.

The Tracking Instrumentation Subsystem (TIS) can simultaneously identify and track up to eight high performance aircraft and 12 additional aircraft and transmit this information to a master station, which processes it and feeds it to the computation subsystem. This Computation & Control Subsystem (CCS) computes aircraft position, heading, altitude, acceleration and attitude from TIS information and that provided by the AIS and passes it to the Display & Debriefing Subsystem (DDS), a control centre where all data is displayed and range activity evaluated in real time.

Initially capable of assimilating Sidewinder and Sparrow performance under simulated firing, the ACMRs are updated to provide the same feedback on newer weapons, such as the Shrike anti-radiation missile. Modifications were carried out on the aircraft that regularly fly the ACM mission, including the Navy's F-5s, F-14s and Air Force F-15s. The first F-5s for the Navy's adversary programme joined VF-43 as the Challengers Detachment, in 1974.

In the meantime, the adversary programme got underway with four T-38As and gradually worked up to operational proficiency by 1975. Home based at Oceana, the VF-43 Det initiated the Fighter Wing One ACM Readiness Program (FFARP), to give it its full title, under the direction of Ops Officer Lt-Cdr Charlie Brun.

The Talons received by the Navy were initially based at NAS Miramar with VF-121, the Pacific Fleet Readiness Air Group. Among the squad-

ron's pilots was Lt Willie Driscoll, one of the Navy's Vietnam aces. Pilots of this calibre devised a tough but satisfying programme for fleet Phantom crews, starting in March 1969 as the 'US Navy Post Graduate Course in Fighter Weapons Tactics and Doctrine'. The name was almost longer than the course — which was soon found to be attempting to cram far too much into four weeks. One week was spent on air-to-ground weapons deployment and three weeks were given over to air-to-air simulated combat. It was the latter phase which demanded more time, and the air-to-ground course was dropped. The all important air combat tuition was subsequently increased to five weeks.

Soon after the course started it was given the snappier name 'Top Gun', despite the fact that the F-4 has never carried fixed guns in Navy service. The course weathered an increased spate of accidents with the steadfast support of Navy top brass, and by the 1972 North Vietnamese offensive was beginning to pay dividends.

The T-38s remained in service at Miramar into the period when the 'Top Gun' course became autonomous in 1972. Two more years were to pass until the first F-5s were introduced by the Navy, by which time the USAF's Air Combat Maneuvering programme was a year old.

The USAF's own study into improved air combat training began in 1970; the Air Force conducted a three-year investigation and held an exhaustive series of interviews 'with every man who had ever seen a MiG in Vietnam'. Each air battle was reconstructed from take-off to landing to provide an invaluable dossier on tactics.

As had happened in Korea with opposing MiG-15s, VNAF MiG-21 pilots tended to employ a recognisable set of manoeuvres in clashes with US air forces. These provided a basis for the tactics which would be employed by friendly aircraft over the ranges — which would also employ the Soviet-style method of ground control. The final 'Red Baron' report was to have far-reaching effects.

The evaluation to find a suitable aircraft to fulfil the 'aggressor' mission was undertaken at the behest of the first commander of the 64th Fighter Weapons Squadron at Nellis, Lt-Col 'Boots' Boothby. The T-38 was found to be the only type in USAF inventory which could adequately duplicate the MiG-21's flight envelope and 20 Talons were loaned from Air Training Command. Boothby's unit went operational on 1 June 1973.

As with the Navy 'Top Gun' aircraft, these Talons could hardly be mistaken for any other in ATC; each one sported a distinctive camouflage scheme and Russian-type ID numbers. The Navy chose to call its basic two camouflage patterns 'Special Scheme 1 and 2', but the Air Force went for more colour, both in application and name — Ghost, Lizard, Patches, Pumpkin, Gomer, Sand, Gray, Blue, Silver and Silver Gray. These

Above left:
Air Force F-5E Aggressor 74-1566. *via Hooks*

Above:
Navy adversary aircraft in their familiar wrap-around colour scheme on a flight out of Miramar, home of 'Top Gun'. *via Hooks*

schemes, designed to match those used by Soviet block air forces, took some time to perfect. The mix did not always come out as planned (there was the infamous Nellis F-5E 'banana' for example, a lurid signal green and day-glo yellow) and pilots were only too aware if they were detailed to fly a T-38/F-5 in the 'wrong' colour scheme over terrain that would show them up.

In their early years the Aggressors also absorbed the expertise of pilots who had seen action in South East Asia. These men were the first instructors who passed their invaluable experience on to a new breed of fighter pilots — the 'post Vietnam' generation.

Good as the T-38 was in establishing the parameters for 'Top Gun' and the Aggressors, it was a little short of the required performance and both services needed something a little 'hotter'. It was logical to use the F-5E, although there were few available in the early 1970s. A substantial US order would have meant diverting aircraft from MAP orders, and there were no plans to do this.

Then came the arms embargo on Vietnam; the termination of aid left 77 F-5Es already earmarked for the SVNAF under MAP. These aircraft found their way into US service and more than meet the new training requirement.

Consequently there were enough F-5Es and Fs to equip three more USAF squadrons for the aggressor role. The 64th was joined at Nellis by the 65th, the second Tactical Fighter Training Aggressor Squadron, under the jurisdiction of 57th Tactical Training Wing, and Nellis also provided trained crews to establish two more squadrons overseas. These were the 26th at Clark AB, Philippines for Pacific Air Force units, and the 527th at Alconbury, UK, for those of USAFE.

A requirement for basing USAF F-5Es overseas posed the problem of how to get them there, it being decided that aggressor aircraft would not be fitted for flight refuelling. Tests were made to package an F-5E for air transportation by C-5 Galaxy and it was found that by partially dismantling the little fighter and lashing it to a pallet, that a C-5 could take no less than eight. Employed for the first time to get the 527th's aircraft to England, the 'eight pack' became the standard method of moving Tiger IIs around the world.

The 527th was activated at Alconbury on 1 April 1976 as part of the 10th TRW, 3rd Air Force. The first eight of the squadron's aircraft arrived on 21 May and the first flight, following re-assembly, inspection and engine ground runs, took place on 1 June. The target date for being fully operational was set for 1 January 1977.

As the only such unit in USAFE, the 527th was tasked with providing disimilar air combat training for all assigned fighter squadrons based in the UK and the continent of Europe. Declared combat ready by the assigned date with 20 F-5Es, the 527th commenced training, initially instructing detachments of F-4s assigned to Europe.

By establishing its own classroom facilities for the all-important pre- and post-mission briefings, the squadron quickly became familiar with the busy UK air traffic environment, its allocated range facilities — and the weather. This not inconsequential factor does tend to make training ultra-realistic, as if it is ever put to the test, the murky skies of Europe are far more likely to be where the enemy is engaged than the crystal clear conditions over the Nevada desert.

But no other exercise area on earth offers fighter pilots the facilities that have been established at Nellis in recent years. As well as the enemy F-5s, the base ACMR offers a host of simulated targets to tax the 'friendly' visiting pilot, and the pattern of training has gradually expanded to encompass the whole spectrum of modern aerial warfare.

It was inevitable that the hard core of Vietnam-experienced pilots would leave the service or be posted to other jobs, and so to maintain the ACM concept it would have to broaden its scope. The enthusiasm for so doing went right to the top echelons of Tactical Air Command and credit for introducing a new phase goes primarily to Gen Robert J. Dixon, commander of TAC in the mid-1970s. Under his guidance was borne 'Red Flag'.

'Red Flag' broadened the aggressor concept to every TAC fighter squadron and beyond; each unit of TAC would henceforth spend part of its time on the Nellis ranges, spreading pilot proficiency more immediately than the previous system of individual pilot training on a relatively small scale, with the pilots passing on their new found skills to squadron colleagues. With the 'Flag' exercises realistic 'on-the-job' training would for one thing be imparted much more quickly. 'Red Flag 75-1' was held at Nellis in November 1975.

Although some changes have taken place in the years since then, the general pattern remains the same — a 10-day 'war' is fought not with guns and missiles but cameras and computers, the players being the world's top fighter pilots. A number of other nations were invited to send representatives to 'Red Flag' for the first time in 1977.

The little F-5 is an integral part of every 'Red Flag'. The home based pilots constitutes Red Force, which Blue Force (the visitors) have to beat, not only in air combat, but by getting through and electronically 'destroying' the ground targets — dummy radar sites, missile batteries, airfield, tanks and vehicle convoys — dispersed throughout the ranges.

But while Nellis has the space (over three million acres) and superb flying weather most of the year, it is considerably short of the typical terrain over which most of its guest air forces (particularly those from Europe) have to fly. It was with this in mind that Nellis instructors crossed the border into Canada to set up the 'Maple Flag' range utilising vast reaches of Alberta — a veritable wilderness of lakes, thousands of hectares of trees, very few people — and weather of the kind that often requires that most basic of

Navy 01 and 02 were the initial F-5Es acquired by that service for the enhanced ACM training programme.

navigation aids, a good pair of eyes.

Establishment of 'Maple Flag', centred on Cold Lake — 'the home of Fighter Weapons' — naturally brought regular participation by local CF-5s. The exercises were started in 1978 and have since grown to rival Nellis to some extent by establishing ground targets. 'Maple Flag' also gained something of a new lease of life for the CF-5, as No 419 Squadron was expanded, and in 1979 the CAF aircraft had become operational with the AIS to give them more realistic feedback on the ranges. The CAF also established its own aggressor element and this is a regular visitor to Nellis and Cold Lake. The CAF assumed full administrative and organisational responsibility for 'Maple Flag 81-7', four CF-5Ds from No 433 and two CF-5Ds from No 419 Squadron taking part.

In recent years it has been realised that any real threat from Warsaw Pact forces would bring high numbers of aircraft into contact with NATO/USAFE squadrons — strengths which cannot be properly simulated by the 40 or so Tiger IIs available at Nellis. 'Red Flag' has therefore fed in more aircraft for Red Force, mostly F-106s and Phantoms, but the similarity of CAF CF-5s to the home based Aggressors has seen these too flying on the opposing side.

The increasingly diverse inventory of Warsaw Pact forces has also raised the question of a replacement for the F-5E and the introduction of a type more representative of high performance Soviet aircraft. It was agreed in principle in 1984 that the Navy and USAF would again procure a

common type for this training and among the aircraft discussed have been the F-20 and the F-16. But the F-20 order would have to be substantially more than the 24 to 36 required by the Navy for Northrop to begin series production; if the world 77-aircraft fleet of the USAF aggressor F-5s were replaced on a one-one basis, the Tigershark may well prove the ideal choice. Other types suggested have included the 'real thing' in the form of a MiG-21 manufactured by LTV Aerospace, and the F-21 Kfir, 12 of which have been leased from IAI for US Navy service starting this year. The Air Force has also stated that it expects to retain its F-5Es well into the 1990s, and as of August 1985 no firm decision had been reached. While a decision on future aggressor aircraft will eventually have to be taken, the Navy and Air Force choice will undoubtedly interest a third party, that of Air Superiority Associates of Sant Fe. Set up by ex-USN pilot Dan Swenson, ASA announced its intention to set up a commercial aggressor school and travel to the customer, rather than have it bear the cost of coming to 'Red Flag'. Swenson and his colleagues also recognise that not every corner of the world is eligible to do so and it is with those operators (which invariably fly the F-5) that ASA would do business. The scheme was approved in principle by the State Department in 1982.

Right:
The business end of one of Alconbury's Aggressor aircraft on display at the 1981 International Air Tattoo at Greenham Common. *Author*

Below:
Artist Keith Ferris designed a number of different schemes for Navy adversary aircraft, as shown on F-5E BuNo 159878 at Miramar on 1 May 1976. All Navy adversary aircraft carry the Fighter Weapons School badge on the fin. *Besecker via Dorr*

13 Towards the Next Decade

As of mid-1985 Northrop remained committed to development of the F-20 Tigershark while concurrently producing the F-5E/F and RF-5E Tiger II for established customers and negotiating with potential new ones. Chinese and Korean production also continues with the result that the F-5 should remain a familiar sight around the globe until the end of the 20th century, and probably beyond. Although the type has not since Vietnam taken a principal role in a shooting war, such is the state of the world that active duty remains a distinct possibility in some areas before final phase-out. Numerous combat sorties have already been flown, albeit on an ad hoc basis.

The ongoing desire of the Shah of Iran to arm himself to the teeth with as much military technology as money could buy resulted in his Air Force receiving a total of 141 F-5Es and 28 F-5Fs. The majority of these passed into the hands of the servants of the Iranian Islamic Republic when the regime of Ayatollah Khomeini attempted to turn the clock back a thousand years. This, fortunately for Iran, it failed to do and the country was not totally unprepared when, on 22 September 1980, Iraqi forces crossed the border and launched air and artillery strikes in the first phase of the Gulf war.

Reports since then indicate that despite a shortage of spares, a selective purging of the armed forces and some defections, the IRAF has maintained a nucleus of what was the world's fourth largest air arm under the Shah at a useful state of readiness. Included in Iran's current inventory are between 50 and 60 F-5Es, which should have been among the easiest to maintain, assuming a careful programme of cannibalisation to offset a shortage of spares and support from outside. The type has been used on air defence duties, although Iran's 500-mile border with its aggressive neighbour has only limited radar coverage due to the premature termination of work on an integrated air defence system purchased from the US under the name 'Seek Sentry'. Consequently, Iraq has been able to mount numerous surprise penetrations of Iranian airspace.

During the spring of 1985 reports from the war zone credited sporadic air activity to both sides, while a war of attrition with heavy casualties brought little tangible success on the ground. Close air support of troops has not been given a high priority by either of the combatants.

Iran was said at that time to be gravely concerned at the vulnerability of Tehran and other urban centres to air attack; approaches made to France and Russia for the supply of ground-to-air missiles indicate that perhaps the serviceability of the IRAF's interceptors — including its F-5 force — has reduced to a dangerous level.

As with Iran, the current status of the North Vietnamese inventory of F-5Es is difficult to determine with any accuracy, although stocks have undoubtedly diminished in the decade since the end of the war. The armed forces of the People's Republic did however strive to maintain a considerable amount of American equipment, including aircraft — which were said to be more popular with flight crews than the Russian machines that otherwise equip the air arm. North Vietnamese pilots were said to be particularly appreciative of the comfortable cockpits and ease of handling of the F-5E and A-37, the two remaining ex-SVNAF jet types.

One fighter regiment composed of MiG-21s and F-5Es was in 1980 commanded by 32-year old Lt-Col Luong The Phuc. In interviews with the Western press, Phuc expressed enthusiasm for the F-5E and A-37, preferring them to all but the most modern of Soviet types — comments which might well be construed as an unsolicited testimonial!

Rumours persist that the North Vietnamese have offered a sizeable part of the captured inventory of F-5Es for sale, with Venezuela among the interested potential buyers. Little evidence has surfaced of such a transaction having been made, however.

In the last two decades, European F-5s have been a familiar sight on the flightlines of the various bases which take it in turn to host the regular tactical weapons meets designed to hone and improve NATO's air defence capability. Invariably dwarfed by all other competing aircraft, the various sub-variants of the F-5 usually make a good showing.

In May 1976 Nos 313 and 315 Squadrons RNethAF hosted the 12th Tactical Weapons Meet

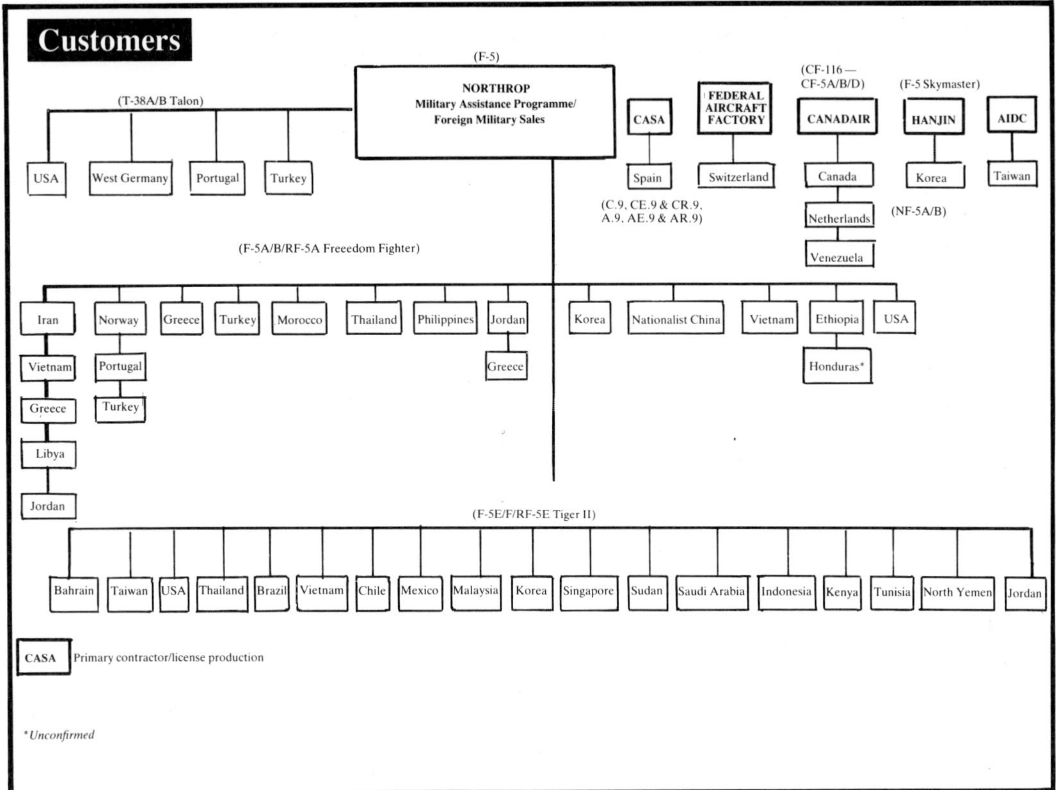

since its inception in 1962, the event at Twenthe marking a change of emphasis. No longer were the TWM competitions between individual nations, but team events, participating forces forming allied formations grouped under two or four Allied Tactical Air Force entries. That year only No 316 Squadron RNethAF actually took part, its NF-5s being part of 2 ATAF.

Among the many NATO joint training exercises which have included Dutch NF-5s, Norwegian F-5As and Canadian CF-5s, Exercise 'Arctic Express' was one in which aircraft from all three nations participated. Held in the early part of 1978 — a busy year — the participants flew from the Norwegian bases of Bodo, Andoya, Banak and Bardufoss on tactical fighter and reconnaissance missions in support of a month-long training programme involving both air and land elements of Allied Command Europe (ACE) and ACE Mobile Force (AMF). In the often sub-zero temperatures, No 717 Squadron RNorAF (RF-5As), No 314 Squadron (RNethAF (NF-5s) and Nos 338 (F-5A) and 433 Squadrons CAF (CF-5/RF-5As) deployed on both sides of the exercise area as parts of Blue and Orange forces, supporting their respective ground units as well as other squadrons of their own air arms and those of the RAF, RN and USAF.

Further F-5 sorties were flown in the tactical reconnaissance exercise 'Best Focus' held at Rygge in May-June 1978. Participants included No 717 Squadron and representatives of the two CAF CF-5 squadrons, the aircraft from which were air-refuelled by one of the CAF CC-137s during the flight from Canada to Norway via Goose Bay.

As well as exercises, individual squadrons of F-5s have made exhange visits to the UK over the years, with units of other nations being the guests of allied air forces under regular and long-standing reciprocal arrangements. Also of course, the Dutch and Norwegians regularly send one or two F-5s to England to participate in air shows such as base open days and the International Air Tattoo.

The 1980s have also seen the phasing-out of early model F-5s as newer aircraft enter service. Norway, Canada and the Netherlands are all due to replace the majority of their F-5s during the current decade. Generally speaking the aircraft has given reliable service but in 1982 the Royal Norwegian AF had to ground up to 60% of its inventory of 80 F-5As and Bs because of cracks in the engine air intake ducting. Investigation apparently revealed uneconomically high estimates of man-hours per aircraft to effect the necessary 'fix' and although these figures were refuted by Northrop, the Norwegians requested that the USAF undertake the work under original MAP agreements. Northrop had known about the cracks for some years and in common with numerous other aircraft which develop cracks after long service, issued routine modification instructions.

A compromise was reached whereby the USAF carried out the work on the F-5As while the Norwegians themselves put the F-5Bs through their own maintenance shops to avoid too much interruption of their training programme. Phase-out of the F-5A from Norwegian service began soon afterwards, as deliveries of the F-16 built up. By 1985 Portugal and Turkey were receiving surplus F-5s from Norway.

Even a small number of second-hand F-5As gives Portugal an increased capability which these days is also exemplified by the Vought A-7. Under a long-overdue modernisation plan, the F-5As are used as interceptors, with the A-7s substantially increasing ground attack capability. All 12 T-38As are also listed as current and Portugal has shown interest in acquiring the F-20. If this happens the F-5As will have been a useful transitional type for pilot conversion to the new single-seaters from Hawthorne.

The F-5A remains an integral part of the Turkish Air Force in the mid-1980s, albeit in small numbers. The THK's 1st and 2nd Tactical Air Forces form the bulk of the 6th ATAF in Southern Europe, responsible for the defence of western and eastern Turkey respectively, while Air Training Command handles OTU and OCU commitments. The 1st TAF's 162nd Jet Squadron at Banirma maintains six F-5As and seven RF-5As

for the dual task of clear weather air defence and short range day reconnaissance, and also supports eight A models and four Bs for conversion training in 'Buzzard' Flight, also stationed at Bandirma. The 2nd TAF includes the 184th Jet Squadron at Diyarbakir for day reconnaissance using 13 RF-5As and one F-5B. All 12 T-38s are believed to be current, the operating unit being Esquadra 201 at Monte Real.

On 5 May 1981 Mexico's Secretary of National Defence confirmed that his country would acquire a batch of 15 F-5Es to equip a single squadron, No 401 at Santa Lucia. The Tiger IIs filled a long-standing need for Mexico to provide herself

Typical of NF-5A updating programmes has been the addition of a 15-round flare/chaff dispenser on the rear fuselage. This machine of No 314 Squadron, RNethAF was a visitor to IAT 85. *Author*

Norway is currently running down its inventory of F-5As and replacing them with the F-16. Seen here is an RF-5A, MAP serial 68-9106. *RNorAF*

Above:
Flugwaffe 059, ex-76-1584, taxying, most probably at Emmen. *P. Bennett/G. Pennick*

Below:
In squadron service, the Swiss aircraft have lately acquired squadron badges, the tiger's head denoting No 11 Squadron. *via Dorr*

with modern combat aircraft, the air force last having operated jet equipment in 1967 when its remaining Vampires were grounded. The F-5E was also the first non-second-hand combat aircraft acquired since the end of World War 2 and it is anticipated that follow-on orders will be placed in due course. No 401 Squadron shares Santa Lucia with No 202 which operates AT-33As, and the present complement is understood to be 10 F-5Es and two F-5Fs.

On 27 March 1985 the Swiss Air Force accepted the last of 110 F-5Es. In nine years the Emmen plant delivered a grand total of 91 airframes to supplement the 19 US-built machines air-lifted to Switzerland by C-5 transport under the F-5E support programme.

On 23 May 1985 it was announced that under an update programme, the Flugwaffe will probably get supplies of the Northrop AN/ALQ-171(V) conformally-mounted ECM system for its F-5s and also a new look-down radar, almost certainly the Emerson APG-69. The May date marked the start of a three-year Swiss participation in the development programme for this new equipment.

The F-5E currently equips six Staffeln, Nos 1 and 13 having converted. Attrition rate appears to have been remarkably good, only two aircraft being known to have been written off since the Tiger II entered inventory.

For Canada the 1980s represent the decade of

the Hornet, the CF-18 being the largest single defence programme to which the country has ever been committed. The Hornet will eventually replace the Voodoo, Starfighter and CF-5 — the latter currently equipping the two original squadrons plus No 219, the OCU. Whether or not the Canadair design will complete a double decade in CAF service remains to be seen, but there is every likelihood that a few examples will still be in service by 1988, most probably continuing in the aggressor role, with perhaps, a secondary reconnaissance duty.

Talon's 25th
In mid 1981 the 20th anniversary of the T-38's service with the USAF had shown substantial cost savings as well as an excellent reliability record. Every service aircraft has an estimated attrition rate which has to be made good to maintain inventory levels and operational readiness. With a figure of 2.2 accidents per 100,000 flying hours, the Talon has enjoyed the best safety record of any supersonic type in USAF inventory — approximately five times better than fighters and about 50% of all other Air Force aircraft. In monetary terms this has meant a saving to the US government of more than $550 million which would otherwise have been allocated to replacement aircraft.

Savings are also rated in man-hours required on maintenance for each hour the aircraft is in the air. For the T-38 this figure has been nine hours on average, nearly a third better than Northrop estimated, and representing a further saving of more than $650 million — or a combined safety and maintenance saving exceeding $1 billion in projected costs. The T-38 has never been the subject of a fleetwide grounding order by the USAF, and in basic design has needed virtually no changes, either during its 15-year production life or since. More than 50,000 pilots have flown the Talon as part of their training and today about 850 are still in use by ATC from a 'still active' total of 960.

The T-38 has been the subject of a number of modifications to tailor it to advanced and conversion training, as already mentioned — but other than those aircraft operated by NASA, there had been no T-38s flown outside military or government jurisdiction, apart from those registered to aerospace companies and used for a variety of duties, including chaseplanes for prototype test flights — certainly none were in the hands of private citizens. All that changed in 1985 with N638TC.

This aggressor-camouflaged beauty is the understandable pride of Chuck Thornton of Van Nuys, California, who built it up from parts of a number of airframes acquired from military surplus over a period of three years. The fuselage of Thornton's aircraft came from a T-38 which had suffered a short landing accident in 1973. The fuselage was put up for sale as scrap and Chuck bought it from a salvage dealer. All he needed then were wings, landing gear, a nose section, seats, canopy . . .

With valuable assistance from Northrop, Chuck acquired the rest of the components, including a set of wings from a T-38 of a production batch earlier than his fuselage. Commonality between production batches presented to problem in marrying the major sections up; with the addition of VHF radio and an F-5 drag chute, the result was an aircraft superior to virtually every stock military example. Chuck incorporated *every* technical order change that Northrop introduced during T-38 production.

Doubtless this will not be the last T-38 to pass into civilian ownership; provided that the purchaser can meet the enormous fuel bills, there will be an increasing number of airframes becoming surplus in the future. Some examples of the T-38/F-5 line have already been acquired for museums, including 61-854, derelict at Pima Air Museum near Tucson, Arizona and currently awaiting restoration, probably by an ex-T-38 instructor. In better condition is 59-4989, the third YF-5A, in the hands of the US Air Force Museum at Dayton, Ohio.

The T-38 actually reached its 25 years from first flight on 10 April 1984; by then the impressive service record had been added to, and by the spring of 1985 the number of flight hours had reached 8,000,000; the loss rate per 100,000 hours was 2.1 and maintenance man-hours had dropped to 7.6 per flight hour. And on 25 September 1984 the F-5F recorded another anniversary, the 10th since its first took to the air in 1974. Celebrated at Williams where it is presently based, 73-889 has lost its early Aggressor scheme and now sports contemporary low visibility grey and reduced contrast national insignia.

An interesting first flight associated with the F-5 was recorded when the Grumman X-29A made its maiden flight on 14 December 1984. Utilising the airframe of the 15th production F-5A (63-8372), the most noticeable feature of this aircraft is the forward-swept wing — the first full scale aircraft so configured to fly in the US. Only the forward fuselage of the Northrop fighter was used to build the prototype, this machine having been in storage at Davis Monthan prior to shipping to Grumman on Long Island for mating with the composite construction wing. Early reports suggest that this unusual marriage will give useful test results, possibly heralding practical application of a revolutionary concept in aerodynamic design.

14 Tigershark

New fighters or variations of existing ones do not by any stretch of the imagination appear overnight, and to offer an uprated version of the F-5E, Northrop had planned since the early days of the N-156F to fly a single-engined version. This was primarily because it was then envisaged that the J85 would eventually reach the limit of its performance, primarily because of its modest proportions. A significant boost in available power would therefore only be possible by increasing the physical size. As retention of two engines would have meant drastic rear fuselage and air intake modifications, Northrop opted to encompass the required thrust in one engine.

The company decided to embark on a private venture derivative of the F-5E initially keeping the family lineage by using the designation F-5G. This was however to be an extremely costly undertaking — in financial year 1981, the project was estimated to carry a price tag of no less than some $140 million, and $42 million was spent in the first quarter of that year alone. It was also anticipated that the F-5G would be priced at least $2 million more than any F-5E.

Northrop received approval for development of the F-5G during the Carter administration when the State Department issued a specification for an Intermediate Export Fighter known as FX, on 4 January 1980. President Carter had revoked the earlier ruling that military aircraft were no longer to be built specifically or modified for export, a move that was subsequently seen to have been naive in the extreme but with good intentions. There would of course be nothing to stop foreign customers (particularly those which had successfully operated the F-5) from continuing to request supplies of US military aircraft.

The FX was thought at that time to meet the President's arms transfer policy, which still maintained that countries would be best served by aircraft tailored to their requirements, their budgets and support facilities. The statement also made it clear that aircraft such as the F-5G would not receive any financial help from the government.

Northrop accepted this proviso primarily because it believed that the success of the F-5E had given it a firm basis for 'follow-on' orders for the F-5G — there was no real reason to believe otherwise at that time.

With the J85 engines having achieved a combined thrust of 10,000lb in the F-5E, raising available output another 5,000lb, would have to come from a single engine, so Northrop considered a number of powerplant options. Choice fell on the

Below:
In striking red and white paintwork, '77-1983' began life as the F-5G, the designation later being changed to F-20 to conform with current US numbering for fighter aircraft and to indicate the type's substantial differences to the F-5E.

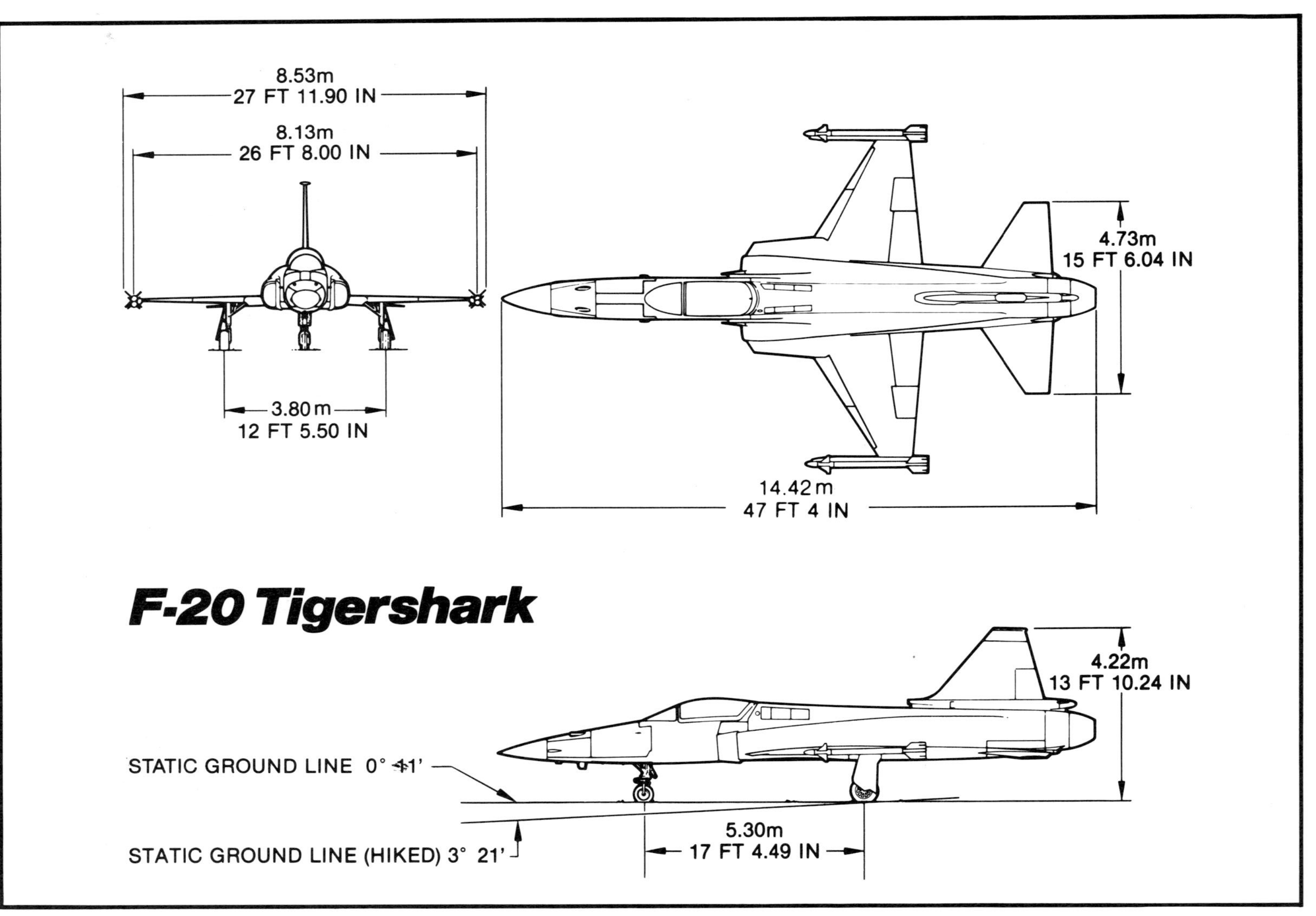

8.53m
27 FT 11.90 IN
8.13m
26 FT 8.00 IN
3.80 m
12 FT 5.50 IN
4.73m
15 FT 6.04 IN
14.42 m
47 FT 4 IN
F-20 Tigershark
4.22m
13 FT 10.24 IN
STATIC GROUND LINE 0° 41'
STATIC GROUND LINE (HIKED) 3° 21'
5.30m
17 FT 4.49 IN

GE YJ101 used in the YF-17, but in its derivative form as the F404, destined for the F-18 Hornet.

To adapt to F-5E to single-engine configuration, considerable modification was necessary: a 5in structural plug accommodated the extra length of the engine; the intakes were enlarged to accept greater mass flow and provide double shock ramps set out from the fuselage to meet projected Mach 2.0 speeds; and the cabin air conditioning system was uprated.

To retain the exceptional handling qualities of the earlier aircraft Northrop also re-contoured the fuselage nose and aft sections and added 'shelves' on each side of the basically circular rear fuselage. These served to reduce development time and generated additional lift at high angles of attack (AOA). The LEX was again enlarged and the wing strengthened to take up to 9g stresses, the tailplane being enlarged by 30%; these and other refinements eliminated any restriction on AOA, roll rate or air-speed.

Almost 50% more visibility was achieved by fitting a new, more bulged canopy and the cockpit display incorporated the latest refinements, includ-

ing digital displays, HUD and HOTAS operation. A wide array of weaponry was envisaged although the twin guns and AIM-9 Sidewinders were retained to keep things simple, especially for those nations which may not have been eligible for more sophisticated weapons delivered by the US.

In its initial F-5G-1 form, the Tigershark used much of the avionics equipment installed in the later F-5Es, including Emerson radar and a GE gyro gunsight. This helped reduce development time and enabled Northrop to fly the first prototype in a little over two years from FX go-ahead. In the meantime various systems were contracted for and were subsequently allocated to four prototypes, the last of which is to fly in 1986. The aim was then to build four flight test vehicles and two static test aircraft. The first flight was due to take place in September 1982, with production aircraft being available by July 1983.

The production target date was reflected in the serial of the first aircraft, 77-1983, applied merely for convenience and the 'crystal ball' department. In the event the company was able to fly the first aircraft with a few weeks to spare, in August 1982.

With its new designation of F-20, and serial number revised to 82-0062 (N4416T), test pilot Russ Scott lifted the sleek new fighter, complete with striking red and white paint scheme, from Edwards AFB on 30 August. Aloft for 40 minutes, Scott took the Tigershark to 40,000ft. He commented 'All test points were accomplished.

82-0062
F-20 Tigershark

Above:
The revised rear-fuselage contours and other salient features are well shown by the second prototype F-20.
via Dorr

We sailed right down the test card. I was most impressed by the Tigershark's power. I had a tough time keeping the speed down to the planned Mach 1.04'.

The GE F404-100 engine had been boosted to 17,000lb of thrust giving a combat thrust-weight ratio of 1.13:1. Northrop stated that the aircraft could accelerate from Mach 0.9 to Mach 1.2 in 29 seconds at 30,000ft, take-off run being 1,500ft. The second flight took place on 2 September, again with Russ Scott in charge; he was up for one hour seven minutes when the F-5F chaseplane ran short of fuel. There were five more flights before the end of September: two on the 3rd (pilots Scott and Darrell Cornell); one on the 4th with Maj James Doolittle, USAF Edwards base project pilot

Top left:
As test flights proceeded, the true potential of the F-20 became obvious. Performance is exceptional, with very low turnround times and a mission capability far in excess of the F-5E. Unfortunately, the MAP countries which it was assumed would buy it have in some instances opted for the F-16, and the Tigershark's 'intermediate' label has been interpreted as 'inferior' in some quarters. *via Dorr*

Centre left:
The first and second prototype F-20s show their ground level attack capability in tests at Edwards in January 1984. *via Dorr*

Bottom left:
In an effort to make it more appealing, Northrop has conducted an exhaustive series of weapons tests to turn an interceptor into a dual purpose weapon — in pilot's terms, a 'mud mover'. *via Dorr*

flying; one on the 6th (Scott); and one on the 7th (again with Scott piloting).

Having cleared Northrop to discuss the F-20 with no less than 43 countries, the first order for four aircraft was placed by Bahrain. But having experienced government resistance in sales support, the launch of production was delayed. The small Bahrain order was not large enough to reverse this decision.

The ever-increasing flight hours accumulated meanwhile, expanded the performance envelope, the first 288 sorties having been with the early F404 giving 16,000lb thrust. Thereafter the GE F404-100 was fitted following the aircraft's debut at the 1983 Paris Salon. This increased performance by a small margin and reduced the thrust-to-weight ratio to 1.1 and increased climb rate from 2.2 minutes to 2.3 minutes from brakes off to 40,000ft.

By April 1983, work was well advanced on Tigershark No 2 (82-0063; N3986B) which was fitted with GE G-200 radar and GE head-up display, Honeywell laser inertial navigation, a Bendix head-down display and Teledyne mission computer. Volvo Flygmotor of Sweden was also watching the progress of the F-20 as the company was anticipating 20% of all GE engine work on F404s sold abroad, having decided to fit a modified version in its planned JAS-39 single-engined fighter.

On balance the F-20's all round performance appeared to make it very attractive to numerous nations wishing to update their defence forces. But it became increasingly obvious that a sale large enough to justify initiating production was going to rely on a substantial buy for US forces first. The tremendous popularity of the F-16 was a factor in the reluctance of the world to opt for Tigersharks — and it is true to say that once the Fighting Falcon entered service, many governments viewed the Tigershark as an 'inferior' aircraft. This in turn stemmed from the FX requirement which had unfortunately labelled the F-5E successor an 'intermediate' fighter. And despite the fact that the F-20 would be more suited to certain nations' needs, the F-16 has become *the* fighter to acquire in the current decade.

Northrop also needs to recoup some of the vast development expenditure — which has already gone past $¾ billion.

Subsequent events did nothing to help potential sales. On 10 October 1984 Darrell Cornell was killed while flying a demonstration for the ROKAF at Suwon. All systems were functioning at the time of the accident, according to the subsequent investigations by Northrop officials and USAF observers. The aircraft was preparing to land, and apparently stalled when Cornell put it into climbing roll with flaps and landing gear extended, the kind of manoeuvre that Northrop's chief test pilot had made famous — anyone who witnessed his incredible display at Farnborough 1984 can attest to that. While inverted the aircraft fell out of the roll and went in from about 1,200ft.

Barely five months later this tragedy was repeated when David Barnes failed to eject from Tigershark No 2 when demonstrating the aircraft at Goose Bay, Labrador prior to flying to France for the 1985 Paris Show. The routine was similar to that flown by Darrell Cornell and again there was apparently little prior warning of anything being amiss.

There followed a series of contradictory announcements from the Pentagon over USAF's requirements for the F-20. Northrop, having decided that the two crashes did not warrant any major modifications, received a number of conflicting statements including 'the Pentagon will entertain the sale of 36 aircraft to Jordan' (February 1982); 'Bahrain will be allowed to purchase advanced US fighters' (spring 1984); 'Thailand wants a squadron of up to 20 F-20As' (early 1984); 'USAF has no plans to buy F-20' (autumn 1984); 'Air National Guard studying possible purchase of F-20' (winter 1984); 'The USAF has no need of the F-20' (November 1984); and 'The USAF is planning to buy at least 100 Tigersharks in FY 1987' (spring 1985).

A lot of this pontification was pending successful flight trials of the SCF-16C, the only other realistic competitor for FX. This limited capability version, with a down-rated engine, closely matches F-20 performance and is favoured by many countries.

In the meantime Northrop flew the third F-20 (N44671) on 12 May 1984 and conducted numerous weapons trials including Sparrow launch, Harpoon anti-shipping missile compatibility tests, various combinations of 'iron' and 'smart' bomb configurations, and pod gun firings.

Below:
Range-boosting tankage was part of the stores added in tests held at Edwards. *via Dorr*

Right:
The cockpit of the F-20 showing the HOTAS, head-up display, and the two digital display screens, which together eliminate a mass of dials and instruments needed for earlier generation fighters. *via Dorr*

F-20
F-20 Tigershark
F-20

Left:
Five Mk 82 iron bombs falling away from F-20 No 2, civil-registered N4416T. *via Dorr*

Inset:
Bombs, missiles and extra gun pods, all have been tested by the F-20. Here the GE 30mm podded gun is fired during a shallow dive. *via Hooks*

Above:
Few who witnessed it will forget the remarkable display of flying skill by the late Darrell Cornell, Northrop Chief Test Pilot, at Farnborough '84. The wing vortices give some idea of the speed with which the aircraft has been hauled into the air immediately after take-off. *Pennick*

The fourth aircraft, being built on production tooling pending that elusive launch order, is to have a further engine uprate to 18,000lb st, more fuel capacity, redesigned leading and trailing edge flaps, with three point drives instead of one, and a larger radar antennae for the GE AN/APG-67 (V) radar — all of which bring the aircraft nearer the equipment and capability of the F-16.

In view of the protracted development of the F-20, Bahrain substituted its autumn 1982 order for four Tigersharks with one for the F-5E in 1985. This covered 10 F-5Es and two F-5Fs, plus 60 AIM-9P Sidewinder AAMs. Under a two-contract deal, Bahrain will also receive F-5 spares and personnel training. The Tiger IIs will be the first combat aircraft acquired by the country's defence force, which was formed in 1977.

The most recent (and encouraging) move is that the F-20 will be the subject of a competition with the F-16. This follows Northrop's proposal to the USAF in April 1985 to sell 396 F-20s at a fixed price of $15 million per aircraft in FY 1986 dollars. General Dynamics' entry will be the specially configured SCF-16C. Northrop on the other hand estimates a saving of some $2,000 million to the DoD if a shared order is confirmed. The outcome appears to be the last chance for the company to build the Tigershark in quantity and although there is little liklihood of it not being able to recoup development costs, the cancellation of an undoubtedly potent aircraft would be an unfitting end to one of the most successful fighter programmes of recent years.

It is also ironic that Northrop is now in a position similar to that when the N-156F was pending production. It is now more than three years since the first Tigershark flew — the parallels with the prototype N-156F are obvious. The difference with the 1985 situation is that the stakes are higher — it will be interesting to witness the outcome.

Appendices

1 Performance Records

T-38A
Jacqueline Cochran, 24 August-12 October 1961

Speed of 1,358.6km/hr (844.2mph) over 15km
   course.
Speed of 1,262.188km/hr (784.337mph) over 100km
   closed circuit.[1]
Speed of 1,095.56km/hr (680.8mph) over 500km
   closed circuit.
Speed of 1,028.99km/hr (640.3mph) over 1,000km
   closed circuit.
Distance of 2,166.77km (1,346.3 miles) over a closed
   circuit course.[2]
Distance of 2,401.78km (1,492.3 miles) in a straight
   line.[3]
Altitude of 17,191.024m (56,071.3ft).
Sustained altitude of 16,841.148m (55,253ft) over a
   15/25km course.

T-38A (61-0849)
Maj Walter F. Daniel, USAF
19 February 1962

Climb to 3,000m (9,843ft) in 35.624 seconds.
Climb to 6,000m (19,685ft) in 51.429 seconds.
Climb to 9,000m (29,528ft) in 64.76 seconds.
Climb to 12,000m (39,370ft) in 95.74 seconds.

Notes:
1: Flown on 6 October 1961.
2: Flown on 15 September 1961, in T-38A 60-551.
3: Flown on 18 September 1961, in T-38A 60-551.

2 Serial Numbers

52-2777	N-102 Fang. Not built and serial actually used in batch of KC-97Ls.
55-6156	N-156 mock-up. Serial number fictitious and reflected sixth development design.
58-1191	YT-38-05-NO Talon (1)
58-1192	YT-38-05-NO Talon (1)
58-1193	YT-38-05 Static test aircraft (1)
58-1194/1197	T-38A-10-NO (4)
59-1594/1601	T-38A-15-NO (8)
59-1602/1606	T-38A-20-NO (5)
59-4987	YF-5A-NO Freedom Fighter (1)
59-4988	YF-5A-NO (1)
59-4989	YF-5A-NO (1)
59-4993	XF-5A-NO Static test; airframe only
60-547/553	T-38A-25-NO (7)
60-554/561	T-38A-30-NO (8)
60-562/596	T-38A-35-NO (35)
60-597/605	Cancelled contract for nine T-38As
61-804/947	T-38A-40-NA (144)
62-3609/3752	T-38A-45-NO (144)
63-8111/8247	T-38A-50-NO (137)
63-8367/8437	F-5A-15-NO (71)
63-8438/8451	F-5B-5-NO (14)
63-13692	F-5B-5-NO (1)
64-13166/13305	T-38A-55-NO (140)
64-13306/13376	F-5A-20-NO (71)
64-13377/13388	F-5B-10-NO (12)
65-10316/10475	T-38A-60-NO (160)
65-10476/10581	F-5A-25-NO (106)
65-10582/10595	F-5B-15-NO (14)
65-13071/13074	F-5B-15-NO (4)
66-4320/4389	T-38A-65-NO (70)
66-8349/8404	T-38A-65-NO (56)
66-9119/9229	F-5A-30-NO (111)
66-9230/9244	F-5B-20-NO (15)
66-14457/14466	F-5A-30-NO (10)
67-14825/14859	T-38A-70-NO (35)
67-14894/14905	F-5A-35-NO (12)
67-14906/14909	F-5B-25-NO (4)
67-14915/14958	T-38A-70-NO (44)
67-21153/21218	F-5A-35-NO (66)
67-21219/21231	RF-5A-35-NO (13)
67-21236/21258	F-5A-35-NO (23)
67-21272/21284	F-5B-25-NO (13)
67-22548/22555	F-5A-35-NO (8)
67-22556/22557	F-5B-25-NO (2)